SECRETS
—— TO ——
SUCCESSION

SECRETS
—— TO ——
SUCCESSION

The PIE Method to Transitioning
Your Family Business

GERARD GUST

Copyright © 2019 by Gerard Gust

19 20 21 22 23   5 4 3 2 1

All rights reserved. No part of this publication may be reproduced, stored in a retrieval system, or transmitted in any form or by any means, electronic, mechanical, photocopying, recording or otherwise, without the prior written permission of the Publisher. For permissions and media inquiries please contact the Publisher at secretstosuccession.com

Published and distributed by Gust Publishing
Special discounts are available on quantity purchases.
For details contact the Publisher at secretstosuccession.com

ISBN: 978-1-9995460-0-7 (paperback)
ISBN: 978-1-9995460-1-4 (EPUB)
ISBN: 978-1-9995460-2-1 (PDF)

Produced by LifeTree Media
lifetreemedia.com

Cover and interior design: Tania Craan
Cover images: iStock

Printed in the United States

CONTENTS

Preface VII

Introduction 1

CHAPTER 1
The Challenges of Succession 5

PART ONE
P is for Priming 13

CHAPTER 2
Priming the Family Business Owner 15

CHAPTER 3
Priming the Successor 27

CHAPTER 4
Priming the Business 53

PART TWO
I is for Implementation 75

CHAPTER 5
Developing the Transition Plan 77

CHAPTER 6
The Transition Team 87

CHAPTER 7
The Shareholders' Agreement 105

CHAPTER 8
Making the Deal 119

PART THREE
E is for Ensuring Success 127

CHAPTER 9
Supporting the Successor 129

CHAPTER 10
Letting Go 143

CHAPTER 11
Managing Conflict 153

CHAPTER 12
Enjoy the Journey 167

CONCLUSION
Achieving Transition Success 173

Afterword by Robert Wolfe 177

Acknowledgements 181

Bibliography 183

Additional Reading 185

About the Author 187

PREFACE

By the time we caught on to it, our controller had embezzled $468,000—close to half a million dollars—from our family's business. The results were devastating, of course, and we worried that we might even have to declare bankruptcy. Shocked by events we thought only occurred on TV dramas, we wondered how we had ended up in this situation. Perhaps it was the result of an all-too trusting ownership that during a time of economic downturn, the right circumstances were created for someone to take advantage of the situation.

Nonetheless, it happened and we had to figure a way out. So, we faced the challenge head on and began working on the solutions that would ultimately save our business. This occurred early on in our succession process while I was still working alongside my dad, training to take over the family business. It was definitely some eye-opening, real-world experience—the kind I never learned from my school textbooks. But when I look back at it now, as daunting as the problem was, it really didn't compare to the challenges we faced throughout the process of transitioning our family business from its first generation of ownership to the second.

The idea of me taking over the family business was my dad's intention ever since I was a child. However, it wasn't until I had worked in the business for over ten years that we had serious discussions about our succession plan. This was around the time he was diagnosed with cancer and he realized it was now or never. At that point we took the first official steps in the long journey of transitioning our family business. We hired consultants, accountants, and lawyers to help us develop our transition plan, and I began doing my own research on family business succession in order to prepare myself.

To my surprise, I found only a handful of books aimed at helping families through this challenging process on Amazon and at the big chain bookstores. How could this be when 90 percent of all businesses in America[1] are family owned?

Most of the content available focused on transitions within larger, corporate family businesses and was written from an outsider's point of view. This content had its own value, of course, but none of it seemed to tackle the issues that smaller family businesses needed help

---

1 "Family-Owned Businesses," https://www.inc.com/encyclopedia/family-owned-businesses.html. Accessed January 2, 2019.

with. It occurred to me that if there were more resources available to help the everyday family business, transition success rates could improve. It is estimated that roughly 30 percent of family businesses succeed in transitioning ownership to a second generation, and only about 12 percent make it to a third.[2]

As we began the transitioning process it seemed like everywhere I turned, I would run into a friend or somebody else who was also going through or planning for succession. They would come to me for guidance, advice, and tips on the subject, almost as if they were gathering the missing pieces to a puzzle. So, while we were still in the midst of our own family business transition, I told myself that this would be a great topic to write a book on, one that would shed light on the real challenges that family businesses face during a transition. Ten years, and countless twists and turns later, this book is the result: one that provides guidance and candid insights into the realities of family business succession.

My intention was to write a guide that others could refer to for information on what to expect, how to plan, and how to navigate through the most common challenges family businesses face during transition. Moreover, I wanted to share a unique perspective on the subject—that of a child who has had the mantle passed down to him by his parent—and to offer practical advice both for current business owners and for their successors by taking both

---

[2] "Family Business Facts," Conway Center for Family Business, https://www.familybusinesscenter.com/resources/family-business-facts/. Accessed January 2, 2019.

Preface

generations' viewpoints into account and finding common ground for them to build on.

Transitioning a family business involves much more than simply transferring the ownership of shares from one person to another. In fact, transferring shares is probably the easiest part of the process. In the matter of transitioning a family business, the key word is indeed "family," and it is in the area of family dynamics that most of the intricacies and complexities of transitioning a business come into play. Finding a way to lead, govern, and work alongside family is the biggest challenge in the process. The lines between parent and child, boss and employee, are blurred, stressed, and tested.

As I reflected on the particular challenges that come with transitioning a family business, it became clearer why there had been so little written on the topic. Not only would it take someone who had gone through the process themself to truly know and understand family business dynamics, but these dynamics can tend to be deeply personal and touchy subjects. Larger family businesses may be able to afford to hire teams of transition experts to help them through the process, but smaller business owners are bootstrappers; they may learn by reading how our family business undertook the process on a more modest level.

The content and strategies described in the book are blended with my own real-life experience, including challenges, failures, and successes. *Secrets to Succession* will give readers a sneak peek—an outline or a map of sorts—to the inner workings of a successful business transition from beginning to end. A book like this would have helped us a great deal if it had been available during our family business succession. I hope that sharing my story and the scenarios we encountered throughout the process will resonate with every family business no matter how big or small.

INTRODUCTION

My involvement in our family business would not have come to pass had my dad not started a property restoration company in 1993. Our business helps those in need during times of unfortunate events such as floods and fire damage. We are the guys who are ready to respond 24/7, clean up the mess, and get people's homes back in order.

I grew up being exposed to the business, and as soon as I reached the capable age of thirteen, I started helping wherever I could. I swept the shop floor, washed the windows, and took out the garbage, which is how my employment in the family business began. At the time, I had no idea that it would continue through high school and university and into the present day. My dad was adamant that I work my way through every position in the company, which meant I learned the business inside and out. In hindsight, this was part of his grand plan to prepare me to take over the business.

As we began the process of transitioning our own family business we started experiencing a set of challenges that pushed our relationship to near breaking point. I expect that many other families face these same challenges and understandably few endure. One of the challenges for us, and likely for most business owners and their successors, was that this was our first time planning a succession, and neither my dad nor I knew what to expect let alone how to prepare. Of course, we heard all the classic lines such as, "It's not easy working with family," or "Most businesses fail during a transition." But until you go through it yourself, you don't understand why people say those things. Like the rest of the family businesses out there, we had to figure it out one step at a time. As much as possible, we relied on outside experts to support us along the way, but in the end, we were the ones who had to make the plan work.

I thought that if family business transitions were as common as they appeared to be, then surely something could be learned from the experiences of others who had gone through one before. Experiences that could help us avoid problems, or at least help us get through them. So, I made it my mission to learn everything I could on the subject. I quickly realized that lack of awareness and traditional transition plans, like the one that was created for us, ignore two very important factors: First, a family must truly be ready to take this step before beginning the process of transitioning ownership. Second, once a plan is in place, a family must still figure out how to navigate

Introduction

through the years before, during, and after the transition. This realization made it obvious that succession is much more than the creation of a transition plan. Rather, it is a process that begins many years prior to a plan's creation and continues even after a plan is in place.

> Succession begins before and continues after a plan for transition.

It was only through experiencing and completing this process that I could draw conclusions about why so many succession attempts fail. Simply put, many family businesses do not treat the topics of family relations, governance, and leadership with the attention they require. Succession tests a family's ability to work together. If the family breaks apart, there is no family business to transition.

For the purpose of this book, I have assumed that you have already chosen a successor for your business and so the strategies and content covered in this book are aimed toward having a single family member take over the business. It is not within the scope of this book to discuss what goes into making that choice, mostly because that is not my experience. Instead I want to focus on the process of succession and how to get through it once you, as exiting owner, have made the decision as to who will succeed you.

During the journey of succession, my dad and I did not have a guide or map like this book to check when we got lost. Instead we took to the open road with nothing more than a compass and an idea of where we wanted to end up. We faced a hundred wrong turns, detours, flat tires, and expensive repair bills, but we finally made it.

I have taken that experience and the knowledge gained from spending $100,000 in fees and costs during our transition to develop what I call the PIE Method to transitioning your family business (see chapter 1). The PIE Method is designed to give the reader a heads up on what to expect so that a family business can anticipate and plan accordingly, thereby increasing their chances of a successful transition.

The letters in the acronym "PIE" stand for the three most important phases for successfully transitioning a family business from one generation to the next: priming, implementation, and ensuring success. The **Priming** phase is the stage where you, the exiting owner, prepare yourself, the business, and the successor to operate as a team and a business that is now family owned and operated. The **Implementation** phase follows once you are ready to begin the transfer of ownership. The final phase is about **Ensuring Success** as the transition of ownership continues to completion. The successor must be prepared to take the reins and demonstrate leadership qualities as the existing owner learns to retreat from the business and adapts to the new circumstances.

Our transition plan was designed to prepare me to take over the business over a ten-year period. However, the experiences and strategies shared here allowed us to expedite and complete the process better than anyone could have anticipated. Though I recognize that each family business has a unique set of challenges to work through, it's imperative that all understand what succession entails and what is required for it to be achieved.

CHAPTER 1

The Challenges of Succession

Before there were multinational corporations, all businesses were family businesses, operating either as sole proprietorships or as cooperatives, where entire families participated in earning their livelihoods from farming, fishing, or a trade. Today, family businesses are the engines of economies worldwide and play an important role providing for their owners and their family members. It is estimated that a whopping 90 percent of US businesses are family run![3]

But what are the traits of these economic powerhouses called "family businesses?" Simply put, they are businesses that have more than one family member working within them and where ownership and control is held by the family. Family businesses are all around us, even if we don't

---

[3] "Family-Owned Businesses," https://www.inc.com/encyclopedia/family-owned-businesses.html. Accessed January 2, 2019.

recognize them as such: they are our local restaurants, grocery stores, plumbing and service companies, product manufacturers, real estate developers, financial services providers, and everything in between. Even some of the largest companies we can name—Walmart, Samsung, Nike—are either owned or controlled by families.[4]

Surprisingly, however, the Conway Center for Family Business in Columbus, Ohio, states that "even though nearly 70% of family businesses would like to pass their business on to the next generation, only 30% will actually be successful at transitioning to the next generation."[5] Why don't most family businesses last beyond the first generation and continue thriving into the second and third generation ownership? Perhaps this is because finding a way to work with family day in and day out, for years or even decades, can be challenging in a way that is unique to the family-run business. And in spite of the many advantages of owning and working within a family-run enterprise (such as familiarity with family members' skill sets and an increased assurance of loyalty and honesty), there are many interpersonal issues and costly forces at work that can tear the fabric that holds a business together.

As someone who has spent almost twenty years working in a family business, and now leads its second generation, I have gained an in-depth look at the dynamics of family

---

[4] "The 21 biggest family-owned businesses in the world," *Business Insider*, https://www.businessinsider.com/the-worlds-21-biggest-family-owned-businesses-2015-7. Accessed January 10, 2019.

[5] "Family Business Facts," Conway Center for Family Business, https://www.familybusinesscenter.com/resources/family-business-facts/. Accessed January 2, 2019.

The Challenges of Succession

relations and the inner workings of the succession process. Despite the seemingly grim facts on failure rates of family business succession that began this chapter, the story of our family business succession is proof positive that it can be done.

Before I get into the details of how to do it successfully, it's worth taking a brief look at the major issues and challenges that family businesses face during succession. I came up with a list of the most common problems we encountered and traced them to four key catalysts that are inherent in many family business transitions. These four factors can be the source of recurring problems and are counterproductive to transition success:

- A lack of succession planning
- Interpersonal issues
- Ineffective business practices
- An inability to stay on track

A Lack of Succession Planning

Research shows that a lack of succession planning accounts for a large percentage of transition failures. It is estimated that only 15 percent of family-owned businesses have an actual plan for succession.[6] Could this lack of planning have something to do with the high rate of succession failure wherein two thirds of family businesses fail at the attempt?

---

6   "The family business sector in 2016: Success and succession," PWC, https://www.pwc.com/gx/en/services/family-business/family-business-survey-2016/succession.html. Accessed January 2, 2019.

You wouldn't start a business without some sort of plan, would you? Actually, I would bet a lot of people do, but all you have to do is look at new venture failure rates to know that this is a bad idea. A recent article in *Fortune* reveals that nine out of ten new start-ups fail.[7] Some of these startup failures can be attributed to a lack of a cohesive, structured business plan. The absence of a succession plan—or the intention of developing one—can result in a lack of clarity and ambiguity as to future direction of the business, its people, the successor, and even the owner.

Interpersonal Issues

Family issues are difficult to avoid. It's easy to say that everyone should just get along, but we all know that's not as easy as it sounds. A family's views and values and how family members interact with one another can have a big impact on those who may one day be involved in the family business. Getting along as one big happy family at home can be difficult when family members work alongside each other every day. Pressure to join the family business and overly ambitious expectations on the part of the parent/existing owner may cause emotional issues, resentment, and even a total distaste for the family business. There can be no family business, let alone a succession, if there is no family to work with.

---

[7] "Why startups fail, according to their founders," *Fortune*, http://fortune.com/2014/09/25/why-startups-fail-according-to-their-founders. Accessed January 2, 2019.

Ineffective Business Practices

A family business is typically borne out of necessity to fill the demands of an owner's quest for freedom, fulfill their ambitions, and achieve financial success. As long as an owner can successfully "steer the ship," then that owner can operate their company on their own terms. Eventually, and when succession is on the horizon, the owner will arrive at a point where they will look to step back from the day-to-day operation of the business. Problems can arise if the business, its people, and its culture are not ready to take on the changes required. The business, its ownership, and the family's legacy will be jeopardized if everyone is unable or unwilling to adapt to an approach that puts the business's best interest first.

An Inability to Stay on Track

The importance of staying on track during the long, drawn-out transition process cannot be underestimated. By staying on track, I mean being able to navigate the speed bumps and roadblocks that hinder the transition process. Disagreements and issues will arise about anything and everything—from business direction to management styles, from performance to compensation—and generational differences will often rear their heads.

Throughout this process there will be times when the exiting owner will wonder if their successor has what it takes. Will the new owner become the leader they have envisioned, embrace the responsibilities of business ownership, and eventually develop the wherewithal to take over the reins of the company?

At the same time, the successor will have their own questions: Will their predecessor be able to one day let go of control over the business? Does the predecessor still have what it takes to run a profitable business? And when will they, the successor, get a chance to lead?

During difficult times both the successor and the exiting owner will question the entire process: Did they make the right decision by trying to transition the business? Are they able to settle their differences and continue working together? Such thoughts and feelings can lead one astray from the transition plan and away from the mission toward succession.

THE PIE METHOD

Certain issues and challenges are more likely to arise and have more impact during key points in the transition process. As a result their solutions will vary. For instance, a lack of succession planning will be less critical if you have only just started working with family and your successor is still many years away from taking over the business. However, if you are expecting to retire in the next few years but have not planned for succession, then much larger issues can and will arise.

Likewise, family issues that come up during the first few years of working together are to be expected as the two of you are still learning to work with one another. On the other hand, family issues that come up years later during the ownership transition stage could carry a much larger impact as both the exiting owner and successor may now be shareholders in the business.

A question like "What does a family business looking to transition into its next generation need to know?" has no simple, foolproof answer. It can only be answered correctly if we understand the particular situation of the family business in question, including what stage of the transition process they are in.

During each stage of succession, the exiting owner and their successor will encounter

> **Identify which stage of the transition process you are in.**

challenges that will need to be addressed in order to avoid the same issues occurring over and over again, and which can inhibit progress through the transition.

During the development of this book I structured the content to help the reader determine their own context in an attempt to better solve their issues and challenges. I assembled the ideas and topics I wanted to cover and began to sort and arrange them into appropriate categories. As the outline was forming, I discovered I could fit everything into three parts. During this process the acronym "PIE" revealed itself. It was perfect. Each phase of the succession process is represented by a letter in what I call the **PIE Method.**

Priming naturally represents the start of the transition. How does a business transition story begin? What is needed, whose involvement will be required, what does the exiting owner and the successor need to know on the road ahead, and how can other involved family members prepare?

Implementation is the development part of the process. By this point, each family member involved has had time to develop their role and has proven their ability to work toward achieving the same goal. Their purpose becomes clearly defined, a plan of attack is drawn up, a team is assembled, and the steps are executed.

Ensuring Success brings us to the end of the story. Transitioning the business is complete—or well on its way. In this phase, each member takes on their new role: the exiting owner makes the transition out of running the business and the successor, or successors, takes over to lead the business into the next generation.

There is a structure and sequence of events that are inherent in all successful family business transitions: prime, implement, and ensure success. The PIE Method is an outline that simplifies the way we think about and approach the topic of family business succession by charting the journey, revealing paths around common challenges and obstacles present at each milestone phase, and helping the reader to understand what may be coming next and how to prepare accordingly. As the saying goes: fail to plan, plan to fail.

PART ONE

P is for Priming

Just as you would prime an engine before starting it up or prime a wall before applying the final coat of paint, the process of transitioning a family business requires priming. The priming stage encompasses all the planning and preparation that is required before a successful transition can begin—the foundation of the process if you will.

The priming phase is the period of time during which a business owner begins to prepare everything required to transition their business to the next generation. There are three key areas that need to be taken into account:

1. Priming the Ownership
2. Priming the Successor
3. Priming the Business

The first step is priming the ownership. It begins with identifying the exiting owner's purpose for transitioning and then gaining their family's support in achieving it. This will allow new roles and expectations to develop within the family. As the involvement of those in the business progresses, their intentions and future within the business are to be made clear to the rest of the family. The ultimate goal of this step is to achieve family harmony—having the family on the same page and in support of each other.

The second step is priming the successor. We will explore the issues that play a role in the development of the business's future leader, including the successor's upbringing, home life, education, and work experience outside and within the family business. This step involves the current leader of the business working closely with their soon-to-be partner and each person defining their respective roles in order to maximize benefit for the business.

The third and final step in the priming phase takes the actual business into consideration. It involves determining how the business will need to adapt to accommodate the transition of leadership. Its structure, management, and business approach will need to be addressed in order to support the transition process.

In the priming phase each of these steps should be embarked upon before the actual transition of ownership can begin.

CHAPTER 2

Priming the Family Business Owner

THE FIRST STEP TOWARD the goal of succession is priming the ownership—in this case the business owner, their spouse, and the family as a whole. Two key responsibilities for the exiting owner are gaining the family's support for succession and ensuring harmony once the process begins. It is hard to enjoy your business successes if you have interpersonal issues at home, lack your family's support, or disagree with them on a unified goal toward succession. Likewise, it is hard to enjoy family time when there are financial worries or concerns about the business's performance.

We endured some difficulties in our succession journey—times when business troubles strained familial relationships or when family friction affected the business. This is precisely why the family's role during the transition process needs to be taken into account if you, the exiting owner, are to pass the role of leader to your successor. At the end of the day, there is no family business without the family at your side.

Clarify Your Purpose

It all begins with you, the exiting owner, and your purpose. As the leader of the business and leader of the family, you set the pace for what is best for both the business and family alike, which is why your purpose must be clear before you can start enlisting your family's support. It is this purpose that will be the foundation that holds everything together, that will bind you and your family together, so that you are all focused on the end goal of succession. Ask yourself, then, what is your reason for transitioning ownership of your family business?

Every business owner has their own unique reason, and usually they have more than one. However, I've learned that there are two foundational reasons a business owner wants to groom a successor to take over the family business.

1. The owner needs an exit strategy that ensures their business legacy continues. Whether for reasons of age, illness, or other unforeseen circumstances, they wish to extract the value of their business—perhaps in the form of a retirement plan—while also providing a plan for the business's future. By transitioning the business within their family they are able to maintain control, choose the speed at which they wish to step away, keep the assets

within the family, and ensure that their legacy lives on with future generations.

2. They want to give their successor an opportunity to earn a good living while working in the business, and hopefully to become the owner in the future. Bringing the successor into the business ensures that both parties will work together to grow and operate the company. Meanwhile the successor is learning about the business, earning a living, and preparing to become the new leader.

I believe both of these reasons will always play a part in making the decision to transition a family business. In my dad's case, discovering he was ill underscored the necessity of putting his succession plans into action. Most of all he wanted to ensure that I had the opportunity for a successful future and to do that, he needed to take pre-emptive action.

Of course most parents want to see their children succeed. Naturally they would do anything within their means to help that become a reality. Most of the time the support and opportunities that parents offer their children eventually come back around, as the younger generation reaches a position where they can return the favour in whatever manner they can. In this scenario, the direct benefit to the business-owning parent is that an exit strategy and possible retirement plan are created as their child takes over the business. A win-win.

Whichever of the above reasons for transitioning you may relate to the most, in the best case both reasons should be critical motivators toward transition success. To see your business move on from one generation to the next and to see it support your child's family as it did for yours—that itself is a powerful reason. So, find your own purpose for transitioning, make it clear, and actualize it. The clearer your goals are, the easier it will be to gain your family's support throughout the process. The more you and your family are informed the better prepared you will be.

> Clarify your reasons for transitioning the family business.

Establish a Time Frame

After identifying your purpose, you should begin to think about how long the process of succession will take. Establishing a time frame will play a part in achieving family support for a unified goal.

Transitioning the ownership of a family business is not something that happens overnight. Instead, it is a process that could take about five to ten years. It is important that everyone involved is on the same page and that they understand that this is going to take many years to achieve, so set the right expectations from the start. Of course, some transitions are much quicker and others take much longer—it all depends on your particular situation.

Sure, the transfer of ownership shares can be completed overnight if needed, whether that's done in the form of a gift, a sale, or upon death. But that is not what we are talking about in this book. Instead we are exploring a gradual transfer of ownership that allows enough time for you, the exiting owner, to extract value from the business, for you and your successor to learn to work together to prepare your successor for leadership, and for you to begin the process of letting go and ensure the business's long-term stability. A period of five to ten years gives you the time required. We will examine this part in further detail later in the book.

The length of the ownership transition period will largely depend on how well the priming phase is executed. Note that the time frame of five to ten years I am talking about refers only to the period of transitioning ownership and does not take into account the time that is required to reach the stage at which you are ready to start transferring ownership. For example, if it takes you five years to complete the priming phase: attaining and maintaining family support, grooming your successor, and getting the business ready for succession, then realistically the entire process will take closer to ten to fifteen years.

Let's look at two different scenarios so we can see how the timing of the transition process can differ.

In the first scenario imagine that you bring your successor into the business when they're at a young age, say sixteen. They work in the business throughout the rest of their teenage years and into their twenties. By the time you choose to start the transition process, they are in their late twenties or early thirties. They have already had over ten years of work experience within the business, including time spent working at other jobs or attending school.

The second scenario follows a different path: your successor goes to school and works at other jobs but is not brought into the family business at a young age. They may have outside work experience that allows them to develop business skills, but they are unfamiliar with your specific line of work. By the time you choose to start the transition process, they are in their late twenties or early thirties.

Of these two scenarios, it is clear that scenario one would be the most beneficial to a family business. By the time the owner chooses to transition the family business, the successor will have already learned the business inside and out, making them ready for the transition to begin taking place.

Although scenario two can still work, the successor will not have been exposed to the business as much as the successor in scenario one—or enough to be able to operate within the business immediately. Scenario two may add time to the transition process due to the successor's lack of first-hand experience and knowledge of the family business. Outside of timing issues, scenario two poses another challenge. If your successor wasn't involved in the business from an early age then it might prove more difficult for you to get them interested later on in life, which will delay the process even further.

As you begin planning for succession, think about timing. Evaluate the current state of your family situation, your successor, and your business, and anticipate how long it may take to get all of those moving pieces ready before you can begin to transfer ownership.

If you are fifty-five years old and want to retire by

the age of sixty-five, then this is the time to start planning for the transition process. By this stage in your life your child may be in their twenties, a most opportune time to be primed for the family business. You will need these ten years at least to prepare for when you reach your preferred retirement age. If everything is in line at the end of that ten-year period and your child is ready to take over the business then you can begin the ownership transfer process, which will ultimately provide you with an exit strategy and with retirement income for however long you choose.

For example, my dad got me involved in his property restoration company when I was about thirteen years old. At the time he was fifty years old (fifteen years before his retirement age goal of sixty-five). By the time he reached sixty-two, we were ready to begin the ownership transition, and a ten-year plan was in place to provide him with retirement income for the next decade.

You don't want to spend your planned retired years chained to the business, fixing your successor's mistakes, or rescuing the business from trouble, so take charge of it sooner rather than later. This is one of the reasons the priming phase is the most important part of the transition process. The successor's ability to lead the company on their own will expedite the timeline of your transition if that is what you desire. At the least, it will quickly free you up from the day-to-day operating activities, so that you can get a head start on your retirement, knowing that the business is in good hands and it can function without you.

Gain Your Family's Support

Now that you have an understanding of your purpose for transitioning and the time required to take on this feat, you can begin getting the family on board with your plans for succession. Priming the family means the family as a whole—not simply you and the successor. You will need the continued support of your spouse as well as any other children or other involved family members to achieve overall family and business success.

The first person to consider is your spouse. You need to make sure you have your partner's support in your plans for transitioning the family business. This may seem like an obvious statement, but in some situations a business owner's spouse may object to having the kids involved in the family business. For instance, they may want the child to focus on school or extracurricular activities, or they may feel that the child is not ready to learn about the family business yet. If that is the case, then planning for succession will be a challenge. So first things first, both parents need to be supportive of the kids joining the family business.

Next in line for consideration are your other children, if you have more than one. As I stated in the introduction, this book assumes that you have already chosen a single successor. Some children have zero interest in joining the family business. Consider yourself lucky if you have more than one interested in taking over. Nonetheless, if you are currently unclear about which of your children to choose as your successor then worry not, as most of the following content can easily be applied to multiple children.

Ideally, you will want the support of all your children for your succession plan. It will create a better family climate when discussing business around the home. As a parent, you want to eliminate any chance of the successor being seen as receiving preferential treatment. For the successor, their siblings' resentment can affect their ability or desire to take over the family business. Your job as the parent and business owner is to keep the family peace.

I believe that the process my dad followed for reducing family conflict was a great approach. They say it all starts at the dinner table, and my dad subscribed to this idea by holding regular family meetings at mealtimes. My dad started gauging the interest of me and my sister when we were in our early teenage years, considering if either or both of us would be interested in joining the business.

During these meetings, he would regularly invite us to do some part-time work at the company, an offer that I was happy to take him up on. Although she didn't show the same interest, he kept extending the invitation to my sister.

> **The process of succession starts at the family table.**

It was his way of making sure he wasn't leaving her out or appearing to demonstrate preferential behaviour. Nonetheless no one was surprised when my sister chose a different early career path, working in retail, and then going on to university to study interior design. I mention this to show how she chose to follow her own path. I, on the other hand, showed interest in the family business at an early age; as I mentioned earlier, I was thirteen when I began working in the business.

Those early discussions my dad had with us about our interest in joining the business made the process feel more fair and inclusive when he decided to make me his successor. Years after we graduated from college, the invitation to work at the company was still open to my sister, and it remains open. This is, after all, our family business. There is always a spot for her if she ever chooses to come on board.

Involving your children in family business discussions early on will help you avoid future frustrations. At the same time, though, you need to respect the position of the child who is already involved in the business. At times I would get frustrated when my dad would ask my sister to join the company. It didn't seem fair to me that she might join in even though I had already put in many years ahead of her. But eventually I realized that it wasn't my dad's intent to replace me. He simply wanted to involve his family in the business in some way or another as a means of providing for all of us.

When your children are young, you can have these kinds of discussions at the dinner table but do remember that your children are impressionable at this stage. You want to show the business in the best light possible so avoid bringing too much negative news to the table. Keep the difficult conversations to yourself and your spouse behind closed doors.

As your children get older, your successor will become more involved in the business while those who aren't already involved will likely be less invested. The number of family dinners may also decrease as your children may no longer live at home. This is the time to start holding regular family meetings that give a brief summary of the current state of the business. These meetings will give everyone a chance to hear the latest updates, successes, and opportunities.

Make sure you get the entire family involved, so everyone can be informed of the status of the business. There may be family members not directly involved in the business who may show a lack of interest in these types of meetings, but the health of the family business is still pertinent to them. After all, the family's financial future and estate are largely dependent on the well-being of the business.

Once the plan for your successor to take over the business is accepted by the rest of the family, there may be less of a need to have these family meetings. In our family we meet about once a year, and even then I would say that they are less important to the whole family than they are to the direct shareholders (the exiting owner and the successor). By the time you are grooming your successor, it is likely any other children of yours are on their own career paths and thus less dependent on the family business, which in turn diminishes interest in these meetings.

CHAPTER 3

Priming the Successor

THE PRIMING PHASE for your child begins early on but be aware that this can be a challenging and unclear period. Your children's lives, specifically their environment, experiences, and upbringing, will be crucial factors in their development into adults. As we know, the transition process can take many years to complete, in part because it may take your successor some time to decide that they want to assume the leadership role. Your chances of transitioning your family business are greatly reduced without a willing, competent, and prepared successor. You may have an amazingly well-thought-out plan and support team, but without a suitable heir it simply will not work.

For this reason, much of this stage is doing everything in your

> Transitioning the business requires a willing and suitable successor.

power to support and guide your child through their own decision-making process without ignoring or squashing other opportunities they are interested in. If your child is still in their teenage years, then this section will be especially helpful as I share my experiences throughout those formative years that helped me and my dad reach transition success.

If you are thinking about retirement options, then it may follow that you would want to involve your children in the business so they can take it over and you can protect your legacy and financial investment. But you cannot expect your child to make such a serious decision at a young age. Gauging their interest in taking over the business may be more difficult when your child is sixteen or eighteen or even twenty than it may be when they are thirty. This is a decision that they will deliberate over many years, so that one day they have the confidence to say "Yes! This is what I want to do with my life." You will need to have some patience during this period in their life. First, spark their interest in joining the family business. Next, keep that interest alive, so that they feel assured in making the choice that running the family business is what they want for their future.

Spark your heir's interest in the business and keep it alive.

There are three critical areas in your child's life and upbringing that can greatly affect their chances of becoming your successor: home life, education, and work experience.

Home Life

During their teenage years, if not earlier, your child may start to think about what they want to do with their life. The thoughts and ideas they develop during this formative period may increase or decrease the chances of them taking over the business in the future. Remember that though you view your business as important (along with your family, of course), it is the career path that you chose for yourself, and it's your own. Just because you feel passionate about your business does not necessarily mean that your child is going to share those same feelings—at least not right away.

Imagine if you wanted a potential client to buy your product or service. Would you use a pushy approach to get them to buy, or would you be more strategic? The process of making this particular sale—persuading your child to be involved in the family business—is one that could take years. It may take some time for them to realize that joining the family business is a great opportunity.

Your child's perception of the world will likely not be the same as yours, so be wary of coming on too strong. Applying pressure to your child can turn them away from you and, by extension, the business, and potentially steer them down a different life path. A child who feels pushed into the family business may come to resent the business itself. There is absolutely nothing wrong with people making choices that reflect their interests. But there can be a fine line between an individual simply following their passion and rebelling against something they believe is being forced on them. How you engage your child on the subject of your business takes a balanced approach. Rely on your skills of persuasion, reserve judgement, and be patient.

Support their interests in other career paths as they explore their life options. Ask them what they find appealing about other professions, and what they want to achieve or receive from those pursuits. Connect their answers with the family business to illustrate how it can provide similar benefits. With your aid and support, your child may come to the realization that the family business is one they want to work in and eventually take over. But you also need to respect their decision if they choose a different path.

Be aware that what you bring into the house and around your family will have a hand in molding your child's outlook on the family business and their potential role within it. One common mistake family business owners often make is introducing negative business topics to the dinner table. If you are incessantly discussing your daily struggles and hardships over dinner you are painting a picture that may not seem so appealing to your child. Why would any child want to come on board with you if the only image they have of the business is unpleasant?

This isn't to say that your child should always be sheltered from the truth or from the hardships that the business encounters. There is a time and a place for these discussions. Ideally, you'll discuss these matters after they have made the decision to join the family business, not before.

The following is a list of simple things you can do to encourage your child's interest in the business:

- Paint a positive picture when discussing business around your future successor
- Place emphasis on the benefits and freedom of lifestyle that the business provides your entire family
- Support your child's interests and their possible career paths
- Present the idea of joining the family business as a career opportunity as opposed to an obligation
- Teach your child about the inner workings of the business, its departments, and its products or services
- Include them in important company news and events

Here are some actions that would effectively discourage your child from taking an interest in the business:

- Talking negatively about aspects of the business, such as its employees, challenges, customers, and financial problems
- Arguing about business with family members at home
- Dealing with business at home; if you must, do so in a private home office

Since you are running a family business, your home life will likely overlap with your company life at times. When I was growing up, my dad would include the entire family in most of the main company events, such as anniversary and holiday parties. It was important to him to have his family attend as it is for many family business owners. When we were younger, my sister and I would attend these functions regularly. But as we became teenagers, we had more freedom to choose whether or not to go to these events, and at the time we often thought we had better things to do.

Remember that we are still talking about teenagers and young adults at this point. It should not be surprising that young people would rather be out with their friends on a Saturday night than joining their parents at a company dinner. Even if they do have an interest in the business, hanging out with friends is likely going to be a higher priority for them than attending company events. It is one thing to insist that your potential successor attend a company event a few times a year, but forcing them to go to more increases the likelihood of them not wanting to work in the business.

My sister eventually stopped attending these events as she had no real interest in the family business. Although I was interested in the business, there were times I did not feel like going to company events. But my dad insisted. A few times he allowed me to invite my friends along, which made it more fun for me. This was a smart move on my dad's part. The more time I spent around the company, its people, and its culture, the better I understood the business overall.

I share this story because it illustrates how I was not yet mature enough to recognize the value in attending company events, the information I would learn, or the support I gave my dad simply by being there. In hindsight I recognize why it was so important. Although your child may not currently comprehend how participating in the company life will benefit them, you should continue to include them in the business even if it's a small thing like attending company events.

Education
Formal education should be encouraged regardless of the field your child chooses to pursue. Ideally, you may want your child to choose studies in the realm of business such as accounting, finance, or marketing; however, other fields can provide them with skills that translate to the business. If they are interested in the family business, they may choose to enroll in business-oriented programs anyway. Regardless of what they choose to study, the core values they will learn from going through the education system cannot be overestimated. In addition to the knowledge they will gain, they will learn to work well under pressure and handle stress, to meet deadlines, to socialize and work with others, and to prioritize work ethic and dedication—skills that are important to succeed in business.

But education comes into play long before your child is ready to go off to college. While the public school system provides a foundation of knowledge, it is not going to teach children valuable life skills that are important for every person regardless of their career path—such as understanding and managing finances, negotiation, and so on. The responsibility for teaching these skill sets often fall on parents.

Long before your child gets to high school and college, you can begin teaching and encouraging them to start thinking more like a businessperson: to be entrepreneurial, to see opportunities and act on them. During their early years, many people will develop some kind of entrepreneurial persona, whether that means collecting and trading hockey cards, or making and selling lemonade. Whether those skills continue to develop or not is a different story. As time goes by, these natural entrepreneurial skills can subside if they're not built upon. You are in a position where you can support the mini entrepreneur in your child.

They don't necessarily need a business degree to think like a businessperson; that's not what I'm getting at here. By all means, if your child is musically inclined then go ahead and encourage them to take lessons and practice their instrument of choice. But you can also teach them about business by introducing them to simple business books, for example. Offering a child a general understanding of how business works—supply and demand, expenses, assets, liabilities, profits—is a gift. I can say with confidence that this knowledge had a great deal in shaping who I have become today.

If you wish for one or more of your children to take over the business then they will eventually need to know how to interpret financial information and understand general business concepts. The sooner they begin learning these skills, the better. Consider which you would prefer: a young adult successor with a solid understanding and a sharp mind for business? Or one with little or no business education or experience? Which family business do you think will be ahead of the game when it comes to the transition?

When I was about fifteen years old my dad gave me a copy of *Rich Dad, Poor Dad*. I had no idea what the book was about, but he told me it would benefit me to read it and get an understanding of why being a businessman was a good choice. By this point in my life, he had already begun teaching me about business in the simple ways, but I still had no specific career aspirations. I wasn't dead set on being a doctor or a pilot or anything of that sort. What I did know was that I was an entrepreneur: from mowing lawns to washing cars, I was always looking for ways to make extra money. This was me being a businessman in my own way. And this is what my dad accomplished by sharing *Rich Dad, Poor Dad* with me.

After I read the book I still had no idea what half of the content meant, but I began to see how the material I did understand applied to my life, and that stuck with me. It didn't take long for me to start talking to my friends about assets and liabilities. None of my friends knew much about business so I became the "business guy" and I found myself regularly sharing my knowledge with them. Naturally I had to maintain my new persona, so I kept buying and reading more business books.

I remember going over to a friend's house one day; his parents were teachers and his two older brothers were both studying computer science in university. On this particular day the eldest brother was home from university. We started talking about the subject of business but he gave me a blank stare when I mentioned focusing on the acquisition of assets instead of liabilities. Granted our positions would have been reversed if he had decided to talk to us about computer programming. Even the simplest of those tech concepts would have brought that same blank stare to my face. But just like that I had embarked on a path that would one day lead to me taking over the family business.

Recognizing the power of the environment, family, and friends on your successor is an important step in understanding that what they are exposed to during their childhood will have a hand in shaping who they become—and education is an important factor. If you have the opportunity to send your child to some form of post-secondary institution, I highly recommend you do so.

During my last couple years in high school I had more freedom to choose classes that interested me, so I took marketing, business, and economics—all the business-relevant courses that were available. Because I was interested in these subjects, I tended to put more effort into these courses. Once I'd graduated from high school, my parents were adamant that I go to college, saying that even if I didn't know what I wanted to do with my life, having a degree would help me later on. My dad, knowing there was a good chance that I would take over the business, suggested I enroll in the business program. Deep down I also knew it was the right choice to make, so the following fall after high school graduation I registered for a college business program and I've never regretted it.

But post-secondary education isn't only about adding to your successor's knowledge bank as I mentioned earlier. During my college years, one of the most important things I learned was how to perform under pressure, whether this meant meeting deadlines, presenting and speaking in front of people, or working in a group to reach a common goal. The business curriculum taught me the basics as well as the more advanced concepts, and that created a solid foundation for my business knowledge that I eventually was able to apply to our family business. But what I am most thankful for is learning how to be persistent, how to work under pressure and deliver, and how to problem solve. These are skills I use almost every day.

Though my school days are behind me, my education has not stopped and never will. I am still an avid reader, but now I spend more time listening to audiobooks because they are a great way to absorb content while I am on the go. Reading and learning from other people, whether they be experts or simply people who have achieved the same goals you are working toward, is also an effective way to increase your knowledge on a topic. I learned this at a very early age: If you want to learn about real estate, go to the top people in the field. If you want to learn about sales or marketing seek out the top people in that field. When it came time to transition our family business, what did my dad and I do? We got our hands on all the family business–related content we could to help us through the process. Simply put, education is a lifelong process and one you should encourage your successor to pursue.

Work Experience

Work experience helps young people learn how to manage money, understand the value of a dollar, and know what a hard day's work is all about. But most importantly, it can help them recognize opportunities that are open to them, whether that is taking over the family business or following a different career path.

When I started working in the family business, I was barely in my teens, and I did all the grunt work you can imagine: sweeping the shop floor, cleaning the bathrooms, taking out the garbage, you name it! At this point I wasn't even working for a paycheque but I did manage to acquire a valuable asset. I had a PlayStation, but I needed a second controller so I could play with my friends when they came over to my house. So I worked in the shop for several weekends, and in return my dad bought me the second controller. This is one of the first examples I can remember of exchanging work and effort for some kind of payment. I kept working, and in exchange I would earn the things I wanted, like a skateboard or a bike. I was starting to learn the value of a dollar, and in turn, my work ethic was developing.

When I was fifteen, my dad encouraged me to get a job at a retail store on the beach promenade close to where we lived at the time. It was all grunt work: sweeping the floor, cleaning the glass, adjusting the displays, taking the garbage out. But at fifteen I didn't have many other skills to offer. Reflecting on that time now, I recall that I didn't hate the job or wish I were doing something else, or even think that I could get better work. It was the best job for my skill and mindset. Afterward, I worked as a dishwasher and then I was hired to wash golf carts at a golf course, a job I considered a step up from the dishwashing position.

As I started earning money, I realized that if I could save all my earnings, I could buy my first car once I turned sixteen. Eventually I did save up enough money to buy my first car, though it was not the one I had dreamed of owning. Once I added the costs of insurance and gas, I didn't have enough for the car I wanted so I went to the car auctions with my dad and ended up buying an old minivan, complete with wood panelling, for six hundred dollars. Though it wasn't my dream vehicle, at least I was able to fit all my friends in it and get around town.

Outside of the summer season, I would work the odd weekend and holiday at the family business, but it wasn't until I graduated from high school that my employment became more permanent. After high school I stopped working summer jobs and started going to college, working at our company on my days off from classes. I did this all through my college years, and for the first time I was making more than minimum wage. But more importantly—and without me knowing—I was also learning how the business operated from the ground up.

I believe it's important for a family business owner to allow and even encourage their child to work at other companies even if it's just for a small period of time. Whether it's during or after high school, or after university or college, they should have the experience of working somewhere where there is no leniency, no preferential treatment, no parents or familiar settings—just a professional work environment. What they reap from that experience is the ability to explore their own path, make their own decisions, and learn on their own outside of the family business. Being free to pursue their own interests for a time will ensure that your successor does not feel like they are existing in your work shadow or that they are locked into one path. By the time your successor does join the family business, they will have had a taste of the outside work force, they will have gained meaningful work experience, and they will have learned the value of a dollar.

Exploring other jobs gave me the ability to get out on my own and experience other responsibilities, which helped put the world of work into perspective. I worked in my family company all through my college years without taking employment elsewhere because I appreciated the opportunity and I knew what I had done all those summers for much less money. I came to value the opportunity of working in my family business, with flexibility around my school schedule, and at a better hourly wage.

The time will eventually arrive when your successor becomes a full-time employee. This may happen after high school, through college, or after post-secondary graduation. Ideally it happens during their early adulthood years, say in their early to mid-twenties. If your child has already spent either the summers or weekends during the school year working in your family business their experience will be helpful in the move to a full or part-time position.

Working together in the business is like the foundation of a building. It will be the strength and support for transitioning your business into its second generation of ownership. This time is important because it will bolster your relationship—not only as coworkers and partners, but also as parent and child. The more the two of you can experience the ups and downs of a business, the better off you will be in the years ahead.

Another reason this initial period of employment in the family business is so important is that it gives the successor the opportunity to learn about the business from the point of view of an employee and not as an owner. They are able to work in various aspects of the business while developing skills they enjoy and are good at. Doing so allows the successor to earn sweat equity with the rest of the company, which in turn helps them earn trust and respect from fellow employees. All of these are qualities that I believe are required of a great leader: the ability to know the business like the back of your hand, the willingness to roll up your sleeves and work when required, and the capacity to lead and motivate your people.

So, as the family business owner who wants to prime your successor to take over the business, what do you need to do to make sure things go according to plan?

Hire Your Successor

First, make sure you hire your child for an existing job rather than creating one for them.

After many years working as the part-time janitor around the company, I was finally hired on as a true employee with real expectations and responsibilities. My job was to assist field technicians. In reality I was a swamper—the lowest position in the company. As the title suggests, I did all the work that no one else wanted to do. The technicians I was paired with were good to me—probably in part because they were good people, but perhaps also because I was the owner's son. However, this didn't mean that they took it easy on me—they still made me do the dirty work.

Although I was still attending college during this time, my class schedule was condensed into a few days per week, and this gave me the time to work at the business. On my days off from school, I was expected to work. This wasn't a made-up position or a make-work project. The timely completion of the restoration projects depended on me showing up.

If possible, find a position similar to the one I held for your child within your family business. One that is essential but not critical to the company, and flexible enough to work with your child's current schedule. The goal is to get your successor working regularly in the company, to involve them in the culture, and teach them how the business operates.

Appoint an Overseer

Next up, appoint a direct supervisor to oversee your child and their work performance. It's important that your child learns to be accountable for their own actions without receiving leniency from you. Having your child report to a supervisor who is not family may ensure they do not get caught up in parent-child dynamics at work.

For example, my friends and I wanted to have some fun on our summer break from school so we planned a camping trip with schoolmates. Although it was short notice, I requested time off work—a Thursday and a Friday so that I could go away for a long weekend. Turns out, I was scheduled to work on those days to ensure the company met the deadline on a large project we were about to close. After my supervisor denied my request I asked my dad if he could help me get the time off—and got a big fat NO.

Long story short, I did end up going on the camping trip, but I didn't leave until Friday after work. The lesson I learned was that even though my dad may have wanted to help me out, it was my supervisor who ultimately made the call. When I returned to work the next week, the time-off policy was made completely clear to me: any future requests for time off required two weeks' notice.

Avoid Nepotism

The above anecdote brings me to my next point: It is important to avoid nepotism as much as possible. And yes, this includes turning down holiday requests from your child who wants to go on a weekend camping trip with his friends.

Avoiding nepotism is especially crucial in the early stages of your child joining the business as all eyes will be on you and your successor and how each of you conducts yourself. If you are susceptible to giving your child preferential treatment then I suggest creating some distance between you and your child in your day to day work. As mentioned above, assign a direct supervisor to handle your successor's work responsibilities. When it comes to payment, make sure you set it at market rates. How much does your company usually pay for the position your successor is filling? That's what you pay your successor. It's that simple. Later on in the transition process, when your successor is either in middle or upper management, you may reconsider this rule of thumb as long as the consequences of doing so will not compromise the business.

Offer Diverse Opportunities

As their time within the company continues, your successor will likely develop the skills and appetite for taking on different positions. This needs to be encouraged systematically.

In my case, I didn't enjoy the frontline manual work that our company did. But I did learn those skills by trying out various positions, going from being a swamper to having my own swamper to running multi-man crews. On the other hand, I was far more excited when I started working in the office, doing the behind-the-scenes work that made everything else possible. I was in my early twenties when I took on this role, which was initially done out of necessity. My dad and his business partner had just split their original business (see chapter 4) because they had contrasting visions for the future of the company, and he needed all the help he could get. I worked in operations for a while, managing the scheduling, the job sites, the field staff, as well as making sure we delivered the promised services to our customers.

When you offer your successor the opportunity to learn how different roles within the company operate, they will develop skills in areas of the business that may be of more interest to them. This process may help them find their niche within the business, something they excel at and want to make their own.

Assign Responsibility

As your child gains familiarity with different aspects of the business and with different roles—and once you deem that they are prepared—put them in charge of a department or an area that you can evaluate closely. Allowing your successor to run their own area of the business will provide you a good gauge of their skill set and abilities. More importantly, it will put them through a scaled-down version of what it takes to run a business. They will learn how to multi-task, manage people, focus on results and not just efforts, and achieve a goal and then set new ones.

After my dad split with his business partner it was like we had a new start-up on our hands. At the time my dad did most of the sales and marketing but as he had his hands full making the new business fully operational we decided that I would help out with some of the sales and marketing activities. Now this was a part of the business I enjoyed. I knew that bringing new revenue into the business would get the company going again so that was my focus. It was tough because I had limited sales knowledge and skills. But I stuck with it. I spent three to four years working in this role (and others) while also acting as my dad's go-to for other important tasks.

A word of caution when allowing your successor to run a department: their actions could have a substantial impact on your business so you should routinely monitor their performance and achievements.

In the years before I was managing the marketing department, the company spent the same amount every year for print marketing. One of my responsibilities included renewing our contract with the local phone book. (Yes, back then print marketing was still effective, so we had several ads in the phone book.) I was put in touch with the phone book's account rep, who made a compelling case for advertising our company on the spine of the book. Our company logo ended up on the spine of about 60 percent of all books printed in our city, and along with it came a bill for a hundred thousand dollars! Perhaps I overlooked the fine print due to my inexperience or I didn't interpret correctly the details of the sales pitch, but regardless the company was on the hook for the bill. After much negotiation, I was able to bring down the price to a discounted rate. The upside is that from that point on, I was a lot more careful with the company's marketing budget. In the early years of the transition, the family business owner should always keep close tabs on their successor's performance and limit the decisions that can be made without the owner's approval.

Over a period of about eight years I worked in every position in the company and gained a great deal of business experience while at the same time finishing my college education. By the time I was twenty-six, I was working alongside my dad and the rest of the management team. The opportunity came up for me to take on the position of controller. I managed accounts payable, receivables, cash flows, and payroll. My main focus was making the company as efficient as possible, "right sizing" as I put it: trimming the fat and trying to grow the bottom line. This experience gave me insight into the inner workings of the company that I had not seen before and enabled me to become a thorough business manager and owner.

After two years as controller, I hired someone else to manage the daily administration and accounting work and the day-to-day financial tasks, but since the embezzlement years ago I handle all the top-level controlling responsibilities. From there, I became the general manager. In this new position, I was able to alleviate much of my dad's workload to the point that his presence was required less and less. This is the home stretch portion of the succession journey.

The time it takes to get to the home stretch will depend on two key factors: the successor's ability and willingness to take the business forward, and the exiting owner's ability and willingness to let go of the reins. By the time you, the exiting owner, gets to this stage—which may take five, ten, or fifteen years—your focus will change from growing the business to transitioning it to your successor. You can begin to put the responsibility of running the business and planning its future growth and direction in the hands of your successor while ensuring that you are leaving behind a sustainable business for the second generation. I will talk more about this stage in part two, the implementation phase.

During this period of working alongside your successor, make sure you do everything possible to create a positive and successful experience for them. The better this journey goes, the quicker it will expedite the transition timeline. This process comes with potential challenges, so I will offer some suggestions for avoiding them.

Temper Expectations
Remember that when your child is starting out in the business, everything is new to them, so have some patience and set expectations accordingly. This is why I suggested earlier that you place your successor in positions that are well suited for their current skill sets and abilities, and move them up to more demanding roles as they make progress. Taking a systematic approach is also why the succession process can take a long time.

I've seen firsthand that this process can be difficult. A friend was in a family business situation similar to mine. His father had very high expectations for him and it caused tension in their relationship. However, my friend had not started working in his family business at a young age. As a result he did not know the inner workings of the company. He had been hired into a position that was beyond his skill set. Although he and his father did work through his inexperience, his learning curve added extra pressure to their relationship for several years. This could have been avoided if the successor had been hired into the right position and the predecessor's expectations for his progress were aligned accordingly.

Limit Parental Tendencies
As you start working with your successor, treat them the same as you would any other employee. This will reduce

the perception of nepotism that the rest of the staff may have (an important piece of advice I shared earlier), while reducing parent-child tension. If you behave like a parent in the office, your successor may feel they will never be viewed as anything but a child. Remember that work time is not family time, so you should both act professionally toward each other and respect the other's position in the company. Of course, it is important to keep a united front whenever possible, and this is something that you both will have to work on. I would even go as far as to suggest discussing this issue with your successor ahead of time, so that when you do have an argument, you can still present a sense of solidarity to the rest of your team. A family business that is divided shakes the foundations of the company, seeding uncertainty and doubt in your staff's minds.

Around the halfway point of the phase when my dad and I worked more closely together, I had gained a good grasp of how the business should operate and began to develop ideas about the way I wanted to manage our projects. There were times when my dad and I publicly argued about how a particular project should be run. It took a few of these instances for my dad and me to realize that we should not be arguing—at least not in public, and definitely not in front of our team. This realization didn't stop our disputes. We had many of them over the years, and even went so far as to make a rule that there would be no negativity or arguing allowed in the office. If either of us, or any of our staff for that matter, was getting heated up, it was understood that we would have to leave the office, go for a walk, and cool off. Over time, the two of you will argue less as you both learn how to work with each other. Likely you are going to have conflict with your child no matter what but it's how you deal with the situation that matters.

Give Your Successor Space
Another key point is to allow your successor their independence. They should have their own sense of identity outside of the family business. Though you'll want to stick to them like glue in the early stages of the process, your child still needs to be able to grow into themselves, which may include having interests and hobbies apart from you and the business. Yes, of course they need to work hard and put in their time in the company but accept that they will need some time outside of that world as well.

When I was first working in the business, I lived with my parents. I would work all day with my dad only to be confronted with more dad time at home. At times all that togetherness was a lot to handle and our patience with each other would be worn thin. I was about twenty-one when I realized I needed my own space, so I moved into a condo I had just bought. Making that move and having my own space outside the business was the best choice as it eliminated the mini struggles we would face at home. We would now drive to work separately, put in our time at the office, and finish the day by going our separate ways. Once I decided to go all in on the business, that's when I started taking my future career seriously.

Growing up in a family business is like growing up on a farm, I would imagine: In both cases, it's common for the kids to be at their parents' disposal 24/7 to tend to what is needed. This can get to young adults and it's normal for them to want to rebel against that authority. When it happens, know that it's a part of growing up. As long as your successor is on track with working and progressing in the business their resistant attitude will likely soften over time.

CHAPTER 4

Priming the Business

It's time to talk about priming the business—in short, getting the business ready to accept its future successor. However this is not yet the point when your child takes over the business. Instead, consider this the step required to prepare your business to accept your successor into its already established operations, a process that may take some years to complete.

In this chapter, we look at the process of building a business that lasts, one that takes into account the best interests of both the business and the family, though I do recognize that sometimes the needs of both can differ greatly. We'll go through the challenges involved in bringing a family member into the business and how to overcome them, how the two of you can work together in the business, what you, the exiting owner, need to do and what your successor needs to do, and how you can both come together in the end.

Build a Business that Lasts

If you were to suddenly leave your business today, would it prosper without you? Would it even be able to operate without you? In essence, you need to prepare your business to function without you and to train your successor and team to keep the business moving forward. You'll be working on your business rather than in it. This is a concept I absorbed after reading Michael Gerber's *The E-Myth*, a practical business guide on essential entrepreneurial skills.

In chapter two we talked about priming the ownership. Here we look at making your company's culture, governance, systems, capacity, and, most importantly, its people ready for the transition.

First, let's look at what differentiates a family business from other business models. Specifically we'll explore the key aspects and practices to reveal some of the challenges you may encounter during the transition process. Even though the business you have now may not include other family members yet, you may be running it as though it does.

Here is a list of some of the characteristics of a family business. Do any of these sound familiar?

- Control and power are within the ownership's family as opposed to being held by shareholders or non-familial partners.
- Company culture is determined and set by the owner's values, ethics, education, and experience.

- There is a less formal approach to everyday operations as employees have a direct line of communication to the owner.
- The owner's personal life and work schedule influence the operations of the business.
- There is a personal sense of care and service with clients and staff.
- Hiring and promotion decisions may be subjective and based on personal relationships with the owner as opposed to performance or objectives.
- Family members may be hired to work in the business ahead of other candidates who may be better suited for the position.
- Company change and progression is limited to the owner's skill set, ability, and vision.

These typical characteristics are not necessarily negative, but they do impose limitations on the business. I share them with you here so you can identify the ones that pertain to your particular company and start working on improving them in ways that will benefit the transition of ownership.

In the process of building a business that lasts, the ability for the business to operate and flourish without dependency on a single person or operator is paramount. The responsibility that once rested on your shoulders alone will now need to be divided and shared not only with your successor but with other key people within the organization, so that as you gradually begin exiting the business, it may continue functioning and growing with its new leadership.

In years past, many family business owners built and ran their companies through trial and error and often without a business plan or any formal business training. They simply created their own companies as a way to provide a job and an income for themselves. This is how my dad started out. He began by taking on odd cleaning and repair jobs, working only with his tools and a truck at his disposal. From there, as demand grew, he hired a helper, then two. Then he needed some office space, and then more people. Fast forward twenty years and we are now a thriving company.

I mention this to illustrate how the needs of a family business owner who is considering transition will likely be much different from the needs of the business owner when they first began. Management practices change, the market changes, demands change, and so on. The business must adapt to the conditions of today's market if it is to keep up. This will entail changes inside the business as well as in the leadership. As the exiting owner, you will need to ask yourself if your business and employees will tolerate a new leader with a similar trial-and-error, learn-as-you-go approach. Or does it require a more trained and focused leader who can build upon existing operations without jeopardizing the business overall. Of course, it is a given that you will not place your successor in the position of new leader until you see that they are fit for it.

What is your vision for your business in the years ahead? What kind of business do you see your successor running? Will it be run similarly to how you ran it? Management styles can differ greatly, and your child's purpose for joining the family business may well be different from your reasons for creating it in the first place.

In my opinion, the best approach is to create a business that has the best traits of both family and non-family organizations. Bring some professionalism to your company and start working toward a better version of your business, one in which you place the company's needs ahead of your own. Consider what the business needs to stabilize and become a solid stand-alone operation that can be run by the second generation. Here are some suggestions to develop a business that lasts.

- Prioritize the business's needs over your own. Are you at the point where the business is no longer growing and innovating? Are you pulling cash out of the business that could be used to reinvest or improve its situation and future productivity?
- Reduce non-critical business expenses, particularly if the business is struggling and these expenses are hindering cash flow or affecting the company in any other negative way.
- Think twice before placing family members into positions for which they may not be qualified or that don't need to exist based on the volume of work available.
- Review employees based on objective criteria such as performance and results, and promote from within.

- Empower your people and use the collective brain power of your team so that your business can grow and develop.
- Break the bottleneck. Do decisions and new ideas go through you and stop there because you are unable to take on a task or explore an idea further? Bottlenecks can result in those ideas dying or being placed on the back burner.
- Delegate tasks that can easily be done by someone else. Think about how you can replace yourself so that the company is less dependent on you.
- Accept change. Understand that new business ideas and management styles may be required to adapt to the changing market.
- Stop or reduce favours such as loans to your staff.

These are a few ways you can help your company move forward and become a business that lasts. The sooner you start putting the company's needs ahead of your own, the faster you will see changes occur that will pay dividends in the future.

Understand that the healthier your business becomes —be it financially or through improved systems and people—the bigger difference you will be able to make moving forward. The more you drain the business of its cash, or fail to reinvest in the business to improve its situation, the farther behind you will fall when trying to

The needs of the company should be the first priority.

transition ownership of the business. Your attention will be split between keeping the business afloat and trying to train your successor.

Make the Tough Decisions

When I started working in the company on a regular basis I was able to see how the company operated. Up to that point most of my job experience had come from working at other non-family-run companies. These places were companies with systems, structures, schedules, expectations, performance reviews—all the things that a "normal" business would have—and where I rarely if ever interacted with the owners. So, when I joined the family business I was surprised to see how my dad was running it.

Those characteristics of family businesses that we talked about earlier? Our business exhibited most, if not all, of those. It was functioning and successful in its own right but I was not used to the informality of its relaxed business practices and approach. With my previous work experience and my college education under my belt, I was impatient. I wanted to change things right away such as implementing new systems and making people, including my dad, accountable for their responsibilities. But I was young and eager and far too inexperienced to know how to properly evaluate the business operations.

My dad made his work schedule fit his lifestyle. He would come into the office in the morning and leave when he felt he had completed all of his work for the day. Of course, I have absolutely nothing against building a business to give you the lifestyle that you want. Heck,

I even practice this today! However, when that type of practice is used, it needs to be supported by a stable business that can operate on its own with systems to support that approach. Our business was not at that point when I joined the team. The systems, and especially the culture, were largely derived from my dad's actions, and his relaxed business approach transferred to our staff. When employees asked to leave work early, as long as they asked politely, my dad would approve their requests with little regard for how their absence would have an impact on the company and its operations.

When someone would fail to show up for work or mess up at a job site, there would be no protocol followed, no employee file to add to—nothing of the sort. Instead, the official response was "just try not to let it happen again." Sure enough, a couple months later, after the incident was forgotten, it would happen again. Some of the staff would mimic my dad's approach to business and leave work early when he wasn't around. This is not optimal if you are trying to build a business that lasts.

As with most family businesses, many of my dad's staff became his friends, making it tougher for him to discipline them when needed. He was the nice guy with the big heart, who would do things like lend money to employees who would promise to pay it back. The employees would eventually leave the company and the loans would never be repaid.

Clearly the examples above are all attributes of a family business that is dependent on its ownership. This is a business in which systems and protocols are nonexistent or unenforced, and in which its employees mirror and adapt to the owner's leadership style. On the other hand, this flexibility and relaxed approach is one of the attractions of working for a family business, but an owner needs to ensure that these attributes are balanced with sustainable business practices.

As I spent more time in the company, I worked on formalizing the business approach, to get it running in less of a mom-and-pop manner. The road that led us to where we are today wasn't easy. As you can imagine, my dad didn't initially welcome his young adult son telling him how to run his business, one he had been running successfully for twenty years. My dad and I butted heads hundreds of times and disagreed on countless issues, but in the end we inched forward in the right direction.

Today, our business is still first and foremost a family business. I have hired many relatives and family friends, but I have also made the tough decisions to remove the ones who were hindering the business. From the outside it may seem like common sense, but it's surprising how many family businesses continue to employ friends and family at the cost of the business itself. Using reasoning along the lines of, "well, he's my nephew, so I want to give him a job" is difficult to defend when there are potentially better candidates outside of the family who could bring more value to the business. By all means, do what you can to help out your family, but uphold your expectations for them to perform according to business standards.

Sometimes in family businesses, performance evaluations, disciplinary actions, and the ability to make downright tough decisions that are best for the business can be sidestepped. It is difficult to dismiss an employee who has helped build and grow the business with you for the last several years, but it is necessary if they are now operating at a mediocre level.

Let me give you an example. Around 2008 the economy took a huge hit, which disrupted businesses across North America and around the world. The financial downturn naturally affected our industry and we felt its effect. We were struggling, yet we kept everyone employed and busy with make-work projects. My dad made an effort to provide all key and long-term employees with full forty-hour work weeks, so that they would not feel the hit we were taking and seek employment elsewhere. Unfortunately, this decision cost the company a great deal of money. At the time we hoped the downturn would be a short-term drop in business but it turned out to be a three-year stint, and the result was six-figure losses.

If the business will not benefit from hiring a family member or keeping them on, then I don't do it. I don't make up positions for family or friends, and I don't employ them at my own cost. In other words, I treat them just like I would treat anyone else—I try to make the best possible decisions for the sake of the company.

With that said, hiring your nephew for the summer isn't likely to kill the business. These family employment decisions are at your discretion. If your business is healthy enough to handle it then help who you can—it can be a great pleasure to do so. Now that our business is much healthier, it can tolerate more than it could during the global economic crisis. Overall, the better the business does, the more I am able to help others and to give back to the community.

But the recession did open my eyes to the realities of business. It taught me that the ability to make tough decisions can make all the difference to the survival of a business. In our case, we could have lost the business if the recession had continued. If the business had gone belly-up, all the good intentions behind keeping our employees would have been for nothing. All of your decisions, including hiring both family and non-family members, need to aid in the goal of moving the business forward.

For better or for worse, the decisions you make early on will dictate how successful, or how challenging, your business transition will be. This is why it is sound advice to follow in the footsteps of those who have already done what you want to achieve. Take a look at the most successful businesses in the world: Many of them, including some of today's giants, like Walmart and Ford, started out as family businesses. However, I will bet you they are not run like they once were and they share few if any of those family business characteristics I mentioned earlier. At some point those businesses started making decisions with the intent of building businesses that last.

Pay attention to their practices. Start running your business in a way that will strengthen it, in a way that will support its longevity for years to come. Make those tough decisions. It's time to set an example for your successor and show them what is required to run a successful business.

Enlist Staff Support

I've talked about some of the key characteristics of family businesses (see p. 54) that could be holding back your company and even slowing down the transition process. If your business shares some of those traits, you can remedy this by adopting a more professional approach. If you are already running a business that demonstrates the professional strategies described above (see p. 57), then you're ahead of the game. The next hurdle is to gain the support of your team as they will be key to helping you during the transition.

There are many moving parts when it comes to building a successful business. At the top of the list is your people. They answer the phones and emails, perform other administrative tasks and services, and generally keep your business running while you're away, day in and day out. As you have noticed, attracting and retaining amazing people, especially in management and key roles, is crucial to building an amazing company.

If your business has been up and running for some time, then you probably have a core group of people your business depends on. If you don't, then it is likely that you are doing all the work and that means you're currently scrambling to find these key people! Your team—the people who have helped you build the business over the years—needs to be taken into account when you're bringing family members into the business. Be aware that your key people may feel slighted or they may simply disapprove of what they see as blind nepotism.

Probably the most common topic of discussion surrounding family businesses is nepotism. Nepotism will likely always be present in one way or another, so avoiding it altogether is not a practical solution. This is, after all, your family business, so in theory your family should benefit from it. That being said, you are also striving to build a business that lasts, so this is a challenge you'll need to handle with care.

To address this challenge, think of your business as a "family business" as soon as you can, even if you don't share blood lines with your initial personnel; the earlier you start embracing this mentality, the more prepared you and your staff will be once your child starts working in the business. Share your business goals and vision for the future with your staff, and let them know that one day you plan on bringing in your child to lead the business into its second generation of ownership.

By sharing your plans as early as possible, you'll have an easier time eliciting your team's support. This is also important in showing your staff that the decisions you make are for their benefit and the continuation of the business. Make clear that you are putting the business's needs first, not your child's, by stating that only when you believe they are ready will your successor be in a position to lead. Your successor will need to earn their stripes, so to speak, before they're in a position of telling the staff what to do. If, on the other hand, you decide to appoint your successor to head the business without advance notice, know that the sudden news will result in some larger issues and you'll find it harder to gain the support of your staff.

Try to understand your employees' mindset by addressing the thoughts and questions they may have. It's acceptable and in fact expected that they are looking out for their own best interests. They will undoubtedly have questions that pertain to their own security and future within the company, and you should be prepared to address questions such as the following:

- Will their plans for moving up in the company and becoming management be hindered now that your child is going to run the business?
- Will they be overlooked for that promotion because your child is getting preferential treatment?
- How does the future look for the company? How does it look for them?
- Will the loyalty and trust they have earned with you, the owner, be lost once your successor takes charge?
- Is your successor the best possible candidate to run the business, or have they simply been appointed because they are the owner's family?

How do you get ahead of these questions and prevent them from developing into larger issues? You need to quash any doubtful thoughts your people may have by regularly involving them in your vision for the company. In reality the only person that will be replaced is you! You need to make that point crystal clear and diffuse as much uncertainty as you can. Explain that the process of training and having your child take over the business is in fact to secure a future for the company—and your employees—and that more opportunities will become available as the business grows and prospers.

Your people need to know that the future and security of the company will not be compromised and that you would not appoint an unprepared candidate to lead the company. Make sure they know that your job in the years ahead is to mold your child into the ideal successor for the company, to ensure that they become the best possible candidate for the position. By emphasizing this point you will gain the support of your people.

Remember that the continued success of your business is reliant on your key people, especially during the later years when the transition process becomes more evident. As your child begins to take on more and more responsibilities, they will need the support and guidance of your key people. These experienced employees will provide insights into the company's functions, its systems, its nitty-gritty inner workings, as well as its culture and employee work ethic, dedication, and accountability. In short, they will be the trainers of your successor. You need to do what's necessary to keep these people around you as they will provide much-needed stability during the transition.

However, regardless of how early you have primed your company for the transition from one leader to the next, key people may react in one of two ways. They will either be reluctant to stay on board, or they will gather round and support you and the business.

Throughout our own journey of transition, I have had first-hand experience with both scenarios. Some of our team members have gone their own way and others have stayed on as a show of loyalty.

I'd like to share the following story for two reasons: The first is to illustrate how even the people closest to you (in this case, my dad's business partner and some of his employees) may not share the same views as you. The second is to demonstrate how you may need time to overcome any business challenges that may arise.

When my dad started the business he was a one-man show. Eventually, as the business grew, he hired more people to help handle the demand for his services. Soon after, he decided to bring in a partner. Ten years later, the company had grown into a multimillion-dollar business with many employees and departments. When I was in my mid-teens, my dad started sharing his ideas for bringing me into the business with his partner and staff. At this point, I was working on and off with my dad, but I still had no idea what I wanted to do. Looking back now, I have to thank my dad for seeing me as the future of the company.

My dad's business partner, however, did not share the same views for the company's future as a family business. As a result my dad and his partner decided to split the company into two entities; the employees, the resources, the clients, and even the vehicles were split equally. My dad's ex-partner then went on to create a company that directly competed with ours. This whole process was one of the most challenging events my dad (and our whole family, for that matter) endured. It was years of dealing with lawyers, mediators, and accountants, followed by years of working to get our business back on track. It took us five years to rebuild and stabilize the business to the place it was before the split. Fortunately, my dad had begun the priming process before the split happened, which meant I was able to help him out.

The summer before the company split began, our family took a road trip to California. During the trip we talked extensively about the family business. At one point the discussion got serious and, frankly, emotional as the rush of fear and uncertainty hit my dad all at once. He pulled the car over and had a heart-to-heart with me and the rest of our family, communicating that he needed my support and help through this process of splitting from his partner. We spent much of the trip planning how the next few years of the transition would play out. The business experience I gained going through the process before and after the split was life changing for me. Though he was still grooming me to one day take over the business, I was now my dad's unofficial partner.

The case of our company split is an extreme first-hand example of how those around you may not support your vision for a family business. With any luck you may just have to deal with an employee or two leaving the company.

Let me give you a positive example of how those around you can support your vision for your family business.

Years prior to the company splitting, I remember having conversations with our employees about me one day taking over. To my surprise, they already seemed to know quite a bit about how the process would look. It was evident that my dad had shared his succession plans with the people in the company, including both frontline employees and management.

I recall one time in particular when I was sixteen—we were remodelling our house, refinishing the part of the basement where my bedroom was. As I have mentioned, our family business is in property restoration, and naturally we hired our team to do the work. I was playing video games in my room with the door open. One of our employees poked his head in, made some chit-chat, and asked why I wasn't helping out with the work so I could learn more about the business. I didn't think much of it at the time, but I later realized that even the frontline employee knew about the plans for my future involvement in the business.

As my involvement with the business grew, that same employee and many others would guide me and show me the ropes, all with smiles on their faces and an eagerness to bring me into the fold. There was a sense of enjoyment or maybe even a self-imposed duty on their parts that I think helped me develop as a leader. Years later, once the split actually occurred, it was no surprise that all those people who had been so supportive in the beginning stuck with us through all the turmoil and uncertainty. These are people who believed in my dad, our family, and our business, and wanted to see us succeed. When we moved to our new warehouse, I was there standing side by side with those same people, moving furniture, painting walls, and setting up what would become our new head office.

To this day, many of those key people who saw me grow up and take over the family business are still with me, and several are now in my top management team. Talk about creating opportunities for your people! Instead of resenting my dad's plans or feeling like they would be passed over, they supported our vision and now hold much more lucrative positions.

To wrap up, you need to start sharing your ideas for a family business with your team as soon as you can. There may be people who will eventually leave to follow their own career aspirations, but more importantly, you will discover those who support you. These are the ones who will likely stay with you for the long haul and who will help transition your business into the next generation of family ownership. With good people in your company, you will be able to better handle unexpected headwinds and business issues that may arise.

The Priming Phase: Key Points

This is the first step in transitioning your family business: It's the time when you make plans and line things up for future succession. Within the priming phase, there are three key areas to address in sequence: the ownership, the successor, and the business. All three are connected, and each is a direct factor in the success or failure of a family business transition. Disregarding even just one of these areas will slow down the transition timeline and reduce your chances for a favourable outcome.

As business owners we sometimes disregard certain things, take things for granted, or simply focus too much on just one area of our lives. Perhaps you are spending all of your time at work, which can cause you to miss out on important family moments. Or the opposite may be true: Too much time is being spent outside of work, causing you to lose sight of the business. Whatever the case may be, you can assess your own situation and adjust accordingly.

The first part of the priming process addresses the ownership. It is important that you realize your own purpose for transitioning and gain your family's support in achieving it, all the while maintaining clear lines of communication about your intentions for the business and the family's involvement. Getting the support of your spouse to bring your child or children into the business is the first step in the process; the transitioning journey will not run as smoothly without it. Next, make it clear to your children that they have the opportunity to be a part of the business, and that the ability to explore it is available to them. If you have multiple children who want to join the business, you should welcome this. However, once a successor has been chosen, that decision should be respected and not questioned. Family harmony is the goal of this phase.

After you've primed the ownership, your focus will shift toward the second part of the priming process: your successor. This is the process where you groom them to become the leader of the business; it should start when they're at a young age and continue into their early adulthood. It encompasses everything from their home life and upbringing, their education and interests, their work experience outside the business, and eventually their working in and learning the family business.

The more attention and effort you put toward priming your child to become the best succession candidate possible, the more time you will save when it comes to the actual ownership transition stage. Of course, a big component of developing a worthy successor is gaining their interest at an early age and having them working in the family business as soon as possible.

The third step is priming the business. Your goal is to have the business ready to accept your successor. While succession may still be years away at this point, the earlier you make it your goal to build a business that will last, the better prepared you will be when succession time comes. This process includes enlisting the support of the company's personnel, from the management staff to the frontline workers, as your team will have a hand in training your successor as they work their way up in the company. This helps to reduce the perception of nepotism and avoid resentment among staff.

In order to develop a business that lasts, some personal benefits and lifestyle-conducive practices may need to change. The business will eventually need to learn to operate without your presence; therefore, the business cannot be solely dependent on you. Proper systems and policies will need to be in place to govern future activities. Begin putting the business first, and make decisions that will be of long-term, communal benefit as opposed to ones that are short-term and personal.

It is during this part of the priming phase that you and your successor will begin working together in the business. This is the time where you are both in essence training and learning how to work together, not as parent and child, but as colleagues and business partners.

PART TWO

I is for Implementation

After you have completed the priming phase, you are now ready to move on to the next step in the transition process: the implementation phase. By this point you have gained your family's support, groomed your successor, prepared the business to accept the transition, and ultimately readied yourself to take the next step. Both you and your successor have the same understanding and share the unified vision of transitioning the family business into the next generation of ownership. This is the part where it all becomes real, and it's time to start putting things into action—in other words, creating and implementing your transition plan.

There are four steps in the implementation phase:

- **STEP ONE:** Create a transition plan tailored to your specific needs and business situation.
- **STEP TWO:** Assemble your transition team—the experts and professionals who will help you through the succession process. There are different roles to be filled within the team, with each member bringing their own expertise and skill set to the table.
- **STEP THREE:** Draft a shareholders' agreement. This is an agreement between partners that will set out the guidelines and governance as to how you and your successor should operate and interact with one another during the transition of ownership.
- **STEP FOUR:** Make the "deal," by which I mean both parties will come to a personal understanding of the transition plan and its process ahead. The aim of this final step is to get the successor to buy into the specifics of the plan.

In essence, the implementation phase gives you a sneak peek as to how the transfer of business ownership could look, whose help you may require, and the documents needed for securing the transition.

CHAPTER 5

Developing the Transition Plan

In this chapter we will take a look at what goes into the making of a transition plan, including how ownership can be transferred, how a business's value is determined, and ultimately how you can create a viable opportunity for both your successor and yourself, the exiting owner. Of course, the needs of a business and its owner can greatly differ from one case to the next, so there is no "one size fits all" approach to the transition process. This is why you should consult and rely on the experience and expertise of your accountant and lawyer to help create the right plan for you and your business.

The people who help you through the transition process is what I call the "transition team." The first two spots that should

Build a qualified transition team when planning for succession.

be filled are those of the accountant and the lawyer. These professionals will be mostly responsible for the creation of your transition plan, and so they are the first to be engaged in the task of beginning the process. Other team members will follow once the plan has been created, but for now, these are the only two contacts you need to have.

Likely one of the first questions that your transition team will ask you is "How long do you want or plan to keep working for?" Your answer will of course determine what the transition plan will look like—in particular its time frame. As you can imagine, a transition plan will differ if you say that you want to keep working for five more years as compared to ten years. In the five-year scenario, the transition will be much faster and probably more aggressive whereas in the ten-year scenario there will be more time available to fulfill the transaction.

Therefore, you should have an idea of how long you envision the transition taking so that your team can develop an appropriate plan. In short, the time frame for your transition plan will set the pace for how quickly or slowly the transition occurs. The time frame not only reflects how long your involvement with the business may last, but also how much or how little income you will receive during the process. For example, a business with a one-million-dollar valuation, set to transition over a ten-year period, could translate into the exiting owner redeeming 10 percent of their ownership shares each year to receive one hundred thousand dollars annually. Of course, it's never quite as simple as that, but this example does give you an idea of how ownership can be gradually transferred.

Transferring Ownership

As you take the initial steps toward the creation of the transition plan, you should also make decisions as to *when* and *how* you want to transfer ownership. The transfer can happen either during your lifetime, after your death, or perhaps both. Occasionally this process begins during an owner's lifetime and concludes after their death. Once that is decided, the method in which ownership is to be transferred needs to be chosen. This can be done by either gifting the business, selling it, using an estate freeze, or using a combination of these approaches.

1. **Gifting the Business:** When an owner gifts their business, the process can be simple. Most of the benefit is received by the successor, as they do not have to pay for their ownership shares. However, this approach does not provide any monetary gain for the exiting owner.

2. **Selling the Business:** This can be the most straightforward approach. A value is placed on the business, and the successor makes the purchase. The exiting owner gets the proceeds, which can fund their retirement, and the successor becomes the new owner. However, this method may pose challenges for the successor as the cost of purchasing the business is likely beyond their financial means at this point.

3. **Using an Estate Freeze:** The basic concept of an estate freeze is that it allows the exiting owner to freeze the current value of their ownership shares

at a given point in time before their successor is brought in. Then, after the appropriate share restructuring is conducted, the successor is able to attain shares that reflect the company's future value. This approach incentivizes the successor to grow the business and increase the value of their own shares. At the same time the exiting owner can maintain control of the business and keep their original shares, which can be redeemed or sold to the successor in the future. There are different types of estate freezes (which I won't go into as this is a subject that lies outside the scope of this book), but whatever form it takes, an estate freeze can provide many benefits, including tax benefits and flexibility, to a transition plan.

For the most part, these are the three methods that your accountant and lawyer will assess and explore when tailoring the right transition plan for your business. It is also not uncommon for ownership transition plans to use a combination of these methods. One reason is that exiting owners want or need value in exchange for the business, so gifting the business in its entirety would not serve their purposes. On the other hand, the cost of acquisition will generally be unfeasible for the successor. Using some combination of these approaches may allow for the successor to get their foot in the door toward business ownership while the exiting owner receives the value they desire.

One thing for the exiting owner to keep in mind is that they should look to find the right balance between maximizing the value they will receive and making sure not to hinder their successor's ability to succeed. In other words, if the purchase price is too high, or the value of the business is not frozen, or the successor is not able to take over the business within a reasonable amount of time, the successor may feel disillusioned with the process, leading to reduced interest and motivation, and ultimately hindering the viability of succession.

Establishing Business Value

Determining your business's value is crucial as it will help determine the best method to transitioning ownership of the business. Your business's value will also give you a realistic assessment of how much your assets are worth and how much money you can potentially expect to receive. There are many approaches to valuing a business, and they can vary from one industry to the next. A brick-and-mortar retail grocery shop will be valued much differently than, say, a tech business.

In the initial stages of exploring a business's value, the owner might ask their accountant for a rough estimate of how much the business may be worth. This is just for the purposes of getting a ballpark figure to better understand the business's current situation. However, it is common—and certainly understandable—for owners to think their businesses are worth more than they are due to sentimental and emotional reasons or perhaps an inability to forgo their own biases. Therefore, the most accurate way of determining a business's value is to hire the services of a third-party business valuator, who will look at factors such as:

- Company assets/liabilities
- Income generated over the past three to five years
- Growth history and projections
- Marketplace and economic conditions
- Recent sales of similar businesses

In some cases, including ours, the amount an owner receives from the business transition is to be their main source of retirement income, and so the owner needs to have an informed idea of their business's value in order to properly plan for retirement. Once a business value is determined, the exiting owner and the successor can begin to plan the method and time frame for transitioning the business. There are several different scenarios exiting owners may find themselves in:

- Their business is worth more than enough for them to retire on, in which case they don't need to worry about supplementing their retirement with other forms of income or investments, or postponing their retirement.
- Their business is worth enough for them to retire on, or the value is an amount that they can make work.

- Their business is not worth enough to solely retire on. They may need to either find other sources of income or investments to supplement the sale of the business, continue working for a longer period of time, or simply make do.

Regardless of how much a business is worth I would assume that most owners are not willing to entirely gift their businesses to their successors. Most people want some sort of monetary return for their investment in building a business. This reality makes transitioning ownership to your successor an obvious choice, as it allows you to step away from the day-to-day activities of actively running the business, and receive the money you need to fund your retirement. However, if you happen to find yourself in either of the last two scenarios described above then this is the opportunity for your team to create a transition plan that better suits your needs.

During the creation of our own transition plan, my dad expressed interest in receiving a set amount over a period of ten years. Because the value of the business could not fully meet his income expectation, we decided to supplement his retirement income with an additional salary for the first several years of the transition while he was still involved in the business, resulting in a transition plan that incorporated the business value as well as an employment component.

Because your successor is unlikely to buy the business outright with their own cash, the transition will be less of a formal sale than if you were to sell the business to an outside party. Therefore, you may have more flexibility when it comes to setting the terms of the transaction—which could better assist your retirement plans. However, as the existing owner, you cannot simply decide how much you want in exchange for the business. It does have to be tied to practical financial factors, which is why I recommend using the business's value as a reality check.

The amount of flexibility available will be determined by your business's financial situation as well as your relationship with your successor. Creating a plan that is too aggressive, or too one-sided, may not yield a successful transition in the long term. This is something that we will revisit later when we discuss making the deal, which requires your successor's buy-in to the plan you are proposing.

Our transition plan took into account not only the value of the business, but also the extra component of employment, which in total equalled the amount of money my dad wanted for his retirement plans. This was an arrangement we were both happy with and it was a relatively accurate reflection of the actual business value. We were both agreeable to the terms and in turn were able to make the deal.

Regardless of all the possible variables and individual business situations, consider your continued involvement in the business and your personal plan for the years ahead. Your transition plan should be clear, motivating for your successor, and feasible for the business's means.

In the end, I believe that because we are dealing with family, we have a natural tendency to want to help each other by whatever means possible. In cases where the business is worth more than enough, the transition plan may be designed to be more favourable to the successor. On the other hand, if the business is not worth enough to provide a comfortable retirement for its owner, perhaps it is the successor who lends a bit of flexibility required to make the plan work.

Much of how a transition plan is structured will come down to how much value you, the exiting owner, want to get out of the business versus how much you want to help your successor. The ideal situation, of course, is finding the right balance that maximizes value for both you and your successor.

CHAPTER 6

The Transition Team

A transition team is the backbone of the transition process and will be a key component to your success. It is a group of people who all share the same goal—helping you transition the business into the next generation of ownership. Each member brings different skill sets and experiences that will stack the odds in your favour. This team is going to be your rock, your shoulder to lean on if and when things get tough or you simply don't know what to do. Ideally, this team will be with you throughout the transition process, so be sure to surround yourself with those you see sticking around for many years.

The benefits of having a transition team include:

- A succession plan created by professionals and experts
- Increased accountability from all members involved

- Team synergy by virtue of a shared goal
- Long-term support and consistency throughout the transition period
- Help with mediation and conflict resolution
- Facilitation of meetings
- Keeping of documentation, records, and meeting notes
- Assurance of proper tax planning, legal filings, ownership transfer, etc.

Your transition team can be composed of two types of members: core members and support members. Your transition plan will determine which team members you may need and how involved they are in the process.

Core Members

The core transition team should be composed of an accountant and a lawyer.

These two members are key because they play a large role in the creation and execution of the transition plan and will likely have the experience of helping other family businesses through the process.

Your current business accountant and lawyer should be able to develop the right plan for your situation as they already know you, your business, and your plans for the future. While these two professionals will bring their own unique values and contributions to the transition process, they also share some of the same responsibilities, which is why they work well together. The core team undertakes some of the most important tasks:

The Accountant
- Helps create a plan for succession
- Helps determine and/or sets the business value
- Gauges the business's financial situation and its ability to support the transition
- Ensures accuracy during the process
- Keeps financial activity in line with laws and regulations
- Safely maintains and updates business records as share ownership changes
- Performs tax planning
- Provides support and conflict resolution

The Lawyer
- Helps create a plan for succession
- Helps determine and/or sets the business value
- Determines if the business ownership needs to be restructured
- Safely maintains and updates business records as share ownership changes
- Performs tax planning
- Ensures legal compliance
- Protects family and business assets
- Creates and/or updates the will or family trust
- Helps create and execute the shareholders' agreement
- Provides support and conflict resolution

The core members' value cannot be overstated: they are the ones who make things happen, from building the plan and setting it in motion to executing share and ownership transfers. They give you peace of mind that all is legally and financially sound during the process. When we started out with our succession plan, we knew virtually nothing about how to transition ownership of the business. We turned to our business accountants, who were of course well versed in the subject. They suggested that we get our business lawyer involved in the process, and that was how we assembled our core team.

Ultimately, the core members will do most of the heavy lifting in the actual planning of how the transition will occur. Once that part is done and the plan is in place, the support team will come into play.

Support Members

Let's look at the other part of the transition team: the support members.

Their role is to further assist the business through the transition process in ways that core members may not be able to. As the name suggests, the support team is composed of those who you may seek additional support from, such as a consultant/coach, a financial planner, your business banker, and so forth. The support team can include anyone who you think could bring value and has a part to play during the business transition.

Of course, not all members will be relied on as much as others. Think of it like this: you have your family doctor that you see on a regular basis for most things, but from time to time you may need to go see a specialist. While your core members serve as your family doctor, these additional support members are those specialists that you may need to see every once in a while.

Keep in mind that the more people you include in the support team, the more opinions and ideas you are going to get. Having input from multiple people could move you in different directions, cause confusion, and slow down the process if they are not united in their purpose. Be sure that whoever you enlist for the team shares the same purpose and vision. Of course, on the other hand, the more experts that you have around you, the more you can leverage their combined experience. I am not discounting this; in fact, I think it's a great idea to have as many competent professionals and experts around you as possible, both before and after the transition. If you have the resources, then by all means, stack your team up.

Now let's take a closer look at the support members:

The Business Consultant/Coach

During this period you will be busy running the business, raising a family, and working with the successor, and now you will have the additional responsibility of transitioning ownership of the business. When your workload becomes too much, a business consultant can help alleviate that pressure.

A good business consultant or coach will help the transition process in the following ways:

- Increasing accountability from the ownership and everyone involved

- Encouraging buy-in and bringing the team closer together
- Taking an objective approach when handling difficult decisions, issues, or disagreements
- Helping develop a plan for growth
- Focusing on set tasks without the need to multi-task
- Helping develop efficiencies within the workforce and day-to-day operations
- Assisting in the implementation of improvements and solutions
- Coaching the involved parties to become better prepared for their new positions
- Sharing their overall expertise and experience in business transitions

When looking for a mentor/coach for your business, you can ask your core members if they know anybody who would be a good addition to the team. Or perhaps you already know someone from an earlier referral. Regardless, at the end of the day, whoever you decide to go with needs sufficient business experience and expertise that you can trust and value.

Remember the business split that occurred between my dad and his partner? It was at this point that my dad decided to bring in a friend of his, a retired consultant, to help coach and provide advice to us. This person had about forty years of business experience in dealing with big oil companies, overseeing and managing thousands of employees, and handling negotiations. He played a large role during the negotiations between my dad and his partner. So, although he was no longer a consultant by trade, he had the skill set to help us with what we needed. Since then, he has earned the title of "coach," not just from my dad and me, but also from the rest of our management team. Naturally, he was a great candidate to help us through the transition as he knew our business and we respected him.

For about a year, our coach worked closely with us; he would come into our office once a week or so to set goals, guide us through challenges, and follow up with us to ensure we were accomplishing what we had set out to do. His presence established a more serious tone to our meetings, helping us transition from the easygoing family business approach to a more professional one, where expectations and accountability were measured. After that first year, our coach was not able to keep consulting for us, and so from that point on we continued on our own. Although we did not have a consultant involved during the entire length of the transitioning process, bringing one on early in the process was enough to help us develop the right habits, which provided crucial support for the rest of our journey.

If you already have a consultant or coach who has been helping you improve the business outside of the transition, you should consider keeping them on during at least some portion of the transition process. They will already be well versed in your operation, its goals, its limitations, and so on, and so they will be able to make the right calls when it comes to your succession plan.

One of the biggest benefits of having a consultant involved during the transitioning process is the ability to create a buffer between you and your successor. For me, it was often better to hear something from our coach than it was to hear it from my dad. Having a coach involved helps replace the parent-child dynamic with an environment of professionalism. Neither you nor your child will want to let the coach down by not delivering on a commitment you made, so accountability will increase all around.

> A good business coach is an effective buffer between the exiting owner and their successor.

As a bonus, when things get tough and you have a disagreement with your child or even your staff, the coach will step in to mediate and remedy the situation. We saw big changes in both my behaviour and my dad's behaviour that resulted in the two of us changing our approaches for the greater good of our relationship and, ultimately, the company.

The Financial Planner

Another expert who is integral to the transition team is the financial planner. As an owner begins extracting value from their business, they will need a plan for how they will manage that money, especially if they want to fund their retirement with this sum (as my dad did). As the transition plan begins to take shape, it will become evident as to how much income an exiting owner can expect to receive. It was at this point in the process that my dad brought in his financial planner to run through the numbers and ensure that they would work with his current and future lifestyle, his investments, and so forth.

Naturally, I did not have as much to do with the planning of my dad's personal finances as with other stages of the transition, but I was privy to the overall plan that was set, which allowed me to understand and support it. Being able to see a financial forecast for the years ahead gave us some clarity as to how things would play out, and thus we were able to make the adjustments required to stay on track. A skilled financial planner will be able to guide the exiting owner through:

- Setting and identifying their financial/retirement goals
- Gaining a realistic view of their finances
- Creating a financial plan or budget for the years ahead
- Tax planning and maximizing the amount of money they will receive
- Managing their money
- Protecting and investing their money
- Planning for unforeseen circumstances
- Ensuring family security

Remember that by this point you are already working on building a business that lasts, and part of that is not using the business as your own personal ATM whenever you need extra cash. During this transition process, you will need to accept that the monetary amounts set in the plan are the amounts you are to expect. This of course means learning to live on a constrained budget and perhaps becoming accustomed to a new financial reality, something I'm sure not many business owners are used to—making it that much more important to seek the guidance of a good financial planner.

The Business Banker

At some point in the future, your successor will need to become a guarantor on your business's bank account and that means that they will have their own relationship with the business banker in order to keep the business running. This can be especially important if your method of transitioning the business involves a direct buyout, where financing may be involved. As you begin to step away from the business and your shares are redeemed, your stake in the business will decrease, which makes it more likely that the bank will need someone else, in this case the successor, to sign and guarantee any future loans, etc. As you can imagine, this transition could be tougher if you wait until the last minute before informing the bank of your plans.

Currently, the bank is familiar with you, the exiting owner; they know your banking history, credit rating, and overall financial standing. This will likely not be the case for your successor. The earlier you bring your business banker into your plans for transitioning the business, the sooner they can help you plan for the upcoming changes.

Now, if your business is completely cash positive and you don't rely on the bank for lending, then perhaps this won't be as crucial for you. But if you are like the other

99 percent of us who do rely on the bank for lines of credit, credit cards, loans, and so forth, then your relationship with the bank will play a role in your transition plan as access to funds is crucial for your operation. Involving the business banker can provide the business owner with the following:

- Support for their business goals and vision
- A simplified or streamlined borrowing process
- Better sourcing of financing, better rates, lower fees, etc.
- Marketplace and industry-specific knowledge
- Review and assessment of their current banking and financial needs
- Connections to other business contacts and experts
- Support for their ongoing business and banking needs

I have seen firsthand the importance of building and maintaining a good relationship with your bank. My dad had a relationship with our business banker for over fifteen years. During that period I only met our banker once or twice. I had no relationship with the bank aside from being the business owner's son. That was all right when I was young and we hadn't begun transitioning the business. At that point I didn't yet understand the value of having a positive relationship with the bank.

A year or so prior to us starting the implementation phase, our banker, who had become my dad's friend over the years, retired, which led to us being assigned to his replacement. By this stage my dad was getting ready to retire and so he wasn't interested in trying to replace or recreate the relationship he had had with our previous banker. Therefore, outside of regular business dealings, my dad didn't develop any solid relationship with our new account manager, and neither did I. There was no true sense of relationship or support, and it showed when it came time to seek help with our loans, lines of credit, and financing. Dealing with the bank suddenly seemed more difficult than it had been in the past. In short, because our account manager had not been brought in to the transition support team, our financial situation became more challenging.

It wasn't long before that account manager moved on to another position, and we were once again assigned a new account manager. Recalling the pain of our recent banking experience—feeling like we were just another number, without any consideration or support—I wanted to make sure that this time it would be different. I took it upon myself to request an account manager who was going to be there for the long haul and with whom I would have the opportunity to build a long-standing relationship in the same way that my dad had with his original account manager.

Our new account manager seemed interested in what we were doing at our company. He was eager to help and also wanted a lasting relationship that would benefit the two of us. I made an effort to speak with him on a regular basis. I brought him up to speed with what my dad and I were doing with the business and how I needed the bank's support throughout the process and in the years ahead. And then the time came when I needed his help: I made a request for an increase in our line of credit and within a few days we received approval for an amount that exceeded what we had asked for. It all happened almost seamlessly.

I had found another member of our support team! Had we not put effort into building that relationship and bringing our account manager in to our transition team, it would have been much more difficult to get our funds requests approved. In this case, our banker wasn't someone we turned to for direct support in transitioning our business, but rather he was there to support us and make the *process* of transitioning easier.

Eventually, the time will come when your successor's ownership stake in the business will reach a level where it will be required that they become a guarantor. At that point your successor, alongside you, will be responsible for unpaid debts borne by the company. In my case this occurred when I reached a 20 percent stake in ownership; however you should check with your own bank as they may have their own requirements. Becoming a guarantor is a big deal for the successor, who now assumes personal responsibility and liability along with ownership. When I became a guarantor, it was terrifying. I had just turned thirty and I was guaranteeing the funds of a multimillion-dollar business.

With the help and guidance of our banker we filled out and submitted the required forms and applications. The bank got back to us and said I had been approved and was now listed as a guarantor. Everything I owned—

my life savings, my shares in the business, the property I owned—was listed on the application as collateral in the event we defaulted on our bank agreements. It was then that the reality of my new role in the business hit me. Talk about a way to really elicit "buy-in" from your successor: This is a surefire way to get it done.

From this point on my dad and I were equally responsible, in a legal sense anyway, for the success or failure of the business. As one of my trusted core team members said during a round table meeting, "welcome to business ownership." As everyone laughed out loud, I nervously chuckled along with them.

Assembling the Team

Now that you're familiar with the transition team and the role of each member, the next step is to decide when to start putting the team together. My recommendation is that you do this as soon as you are ready to move on from the priming phase to implementation.

The team will begin to form naturally as soon as you share your intentions for the transition with your lawyer and/or accountant. In this case the core of your team is already in place; they are simply waiting for your signal to begin working on the transition plan.

Once the core members of your team have been assembled, you can start adding the necessary support members. I recall our first meeting regarding the transition, which took place in our accountant's boardroom. Our accountant had been in discussions with my dad for months, and they had compiled an action plan of how this transition was going to work. At that point the team was bare bones: our accountant, his assistant, my dad, and me.

The next and obvious member of our core transition team was our business lawyer, who had been dealing with my dad and our business for over twenty years. Then my dad brought in his estate/financial planner to help him handle his income schedule for the next ten years during the buyout phase as well as his investments and his overall retirement plans.

Although our "coach" was involved during the early priming stages of the transition process, he had less of a contribution during the actual transition of ownership. As the ownership transition took place years later he was no longer available to consult for us. Thankfully our accountant was able to step up and provide that support for us. He went above and beyond in his role and acted as our advisor, therapist, mediator, and friend, and provided all that was needed to execute the transition. It was clear that he was deeply invested in the success of our business transition.

As I said before, the most important and hardest thing to accomplish during a business transition is for everyone to unite as a family and a business. This process will often test both the exiting owner and their successor, pushing them to the limits of what they think they can handle. An amazing transition team will make all the difference, so never underestimate the value of your team members.

Learn to rely on your transition team members.

The Costs of a Transition Team

All this talk of business consultants, lawyers, and accountants sounds expensive, doesn't it? So let's talk about what you should expect to pay to have a team of experts help transition ownership of your business.

The additional costs of assembling your transition team, at least when it comes to the core members, may not amount to much more than what you are already paying these members. The core members—your lawyer and your accountant—should to some extent already be providing you with their services as part of their regular business functions. Therefore, some of the costs and time required to find and hire these professionals has already been expensed. The difference now is that the lawyer and accountant are required to spend additional time on the project of transitioning the business—and that will result in a fee increase.

Take, for example your accountant. Likely, you are already paying them to do your company's books and provide financial and accounting support. Typically, the only increase will be the cost of developing the transition plan. In our first year of getting the team set up and running, our accounting and legal fees almost doubled as the transition required some specific front-end work. But once our transition plan was drawn up and in place, the accounting fees dropped drastically.

Now we have two meetings a year with our accountant: one for the actual business dealings and the other to review the transition progress. Sure, some extra billable time does accrue during the discussions of transition matters, but the cost is marginal. The same goes for legal fees. You already employ a lawyer to handle the usual legal matters, but when you need to talk to them about the transition, get their advice, develop the shareholders' agreement, or undertake filings of share redemptions, you will be billed for these extra items.

The costs associated with a transition team can vary greatly and they are dependent on the size of your business and the complexity of the transition plan. The larger the company and the more complex the transition plan, the more you can expect the costs to increase. For peace of mind, you can always ask your accountant and lawyer for a ballpark figure as to how much it will initially cost you to develop a transition plan, and then adjust that amount according to your own budget.

When it comes to the costs associated with the support members of the transition team, you have some flexibility as you can control how many members you want on board and how long you retain their services for. After accounting and legal fees, the cost of hiring a consultant/coach is likely the next largest expense over the long term.

Although not every business owner or company can afford to bring in a business consultant, I would encourage you to at least explore the possibility. A consultant may be willing to adapt to your specific budget and situation, and this should be part of the conversation at the outset. Maybe you can work out an arrangement whereby you meet with the consultant once a quarter instead of monthly or weekly. Or, perhaps, you contract them on an as-needed basis for the times when you need specific help, and they only bill you for the time they spend on those specific issues. When the time comes that you feel you need the help of a consultant, be sure to do your research and ask your lawyer and accountant if they can recommend someone who would be a good fit for your particular situation and budget.

Although hiring a good consultant does come with a cost, you should also consider the potential costs and losses associated with a trial and error–type approach. If you are trying to figure things out as you go, you may end up spending a great deal of time and money on things that ultimately don't benefit your business. These headaches can be avoided by getting the assistance and guidance of a consultant/coach.

Other support team members, such as your financial advisor/planner or even your banker, will likely provide the support you need as part of the service they already provide. It is in their interest to see your business continue into the second generation.

There is an initial cost to creating the transition plan and shareholders' agreement, and some yearly maintenance will be needed, but all the extra time spent on your transition is likely to be billed on a per hour basis, depending on how much help you seek. Remember what it is you are trying to achieve and how much it is worth to you and the business. At the end of the day, costs that you find excessive now will likely pale in comparison to the value of successfully completing the transition.

CHAPTER 7

The Shareholders' Agreement

By this stage, the exiting owner and the successor should have a transition plan and a transition team in place. Next is the drafting of a shareholders' agreement (SA), which must happen before the deal between you and your successor is made. If you don't know what a shareholders' agreement is—neither I nor my dad did at first—then you are about to learn why having one is an absolute necessity.

Basically, an SA is an agreement made between the shareholders that outlines how they will work together. It is essentially a set of rules for how the shareholders will be governed and how resolution can be achieved should there ever be disputes among the ownership. Your corporate

> A shareholders' agreement is an absolute necessity.

lawyer should draft the shareholders' agreement. It can include clauses pertaining to areas such as:

- Listing of company shareholders and directors
- Meeting governance and voting processes
- Financial requirements and how profits will be paid out
- Rules around the sale and transfer of shares
- Restrictions on shareholders
- Dispute resolutions and deadlocks
- Transfer of interests upon death
- Life insurance requirements
- How to establish fair market value on company shares
- Non-competes and confidentiality agreements
- Any matters or decisions that would require unanimous consent
- Breach of shareholders' covenants, etc.

An SA can cover many different topics and thus open up a lot of conversations that could lead to disputes over hypothetical situations.

The SA should be created upon the completion of the transition plan as the SA will be needed by the time the final deal is made. The reason for this is that the SA will dictate how your partnership will be governed, and naturally both parties need to agree on these details in order for the transition to work. I like to think of it in the following way: The transition plan tells you what game you are going to play, but the SA tells you the rules of the game. Both are necessary for the game to function.

When the plan was created for our own transition, there were some minor tweaks here and there, but in the end we all agreed on how the transition would unfold. At that time, our accountant advised that we put together an SA to solidify all the details of our agreement. Yet, six months later, my dad and I still hadn't started the process as we didn't think that it was a pressing issue. Our accountant continued to remind us about it, pointing out that a shareholders' agreement would help us understand what to do in the event of a death, that it would lay out how to resolve future disputes, and guide us going forward. Eventually, after many reminders, we decided to get the ball rolling.

> **The shareholders' agreement outlines the rules of the transition plan.**

My dad called up our lawyer and asked him to put together an SA for us. Soon after, we received our SA, which was forty pages long and written in what seemed to me to be another language. It was my first exposure to reading a legal document of this type. I glanced at it and gave a few comments, but overall I found no issues with the SA. Nothing happened for a few more months until our next meeting with our accounting team in early winter. With our accountant acting as both our core and support team, we reviewed some of the general points of the document; aside from some small amendments to be made, it still appeared fine to me.

I had booked a trip to Cancun that was to take place soon after the meeting. A few days before my departure, our lawyer sent back the revised SA, addressing the few things we had discussed. I glanced at it and told my dad I would look at it more carefully when I got back. The night before I was to leave on my trip, I got a call from my dad saying we needed to address the SA before I left. After discussing the importance of the SA with the lawyer, he realized it was a document that needed to be signed and sealed before anything happened to either one of us. Doing this would also solidify the loose ends of the deal, which was essential moving forward.

Given the apparent urgency of the situation, I decided to forgo my trip in favour of addressing the business issues. As much as I wished that the SA could wait until my return, I understood its importance for the business and the transition. A few days later, my dad and I met to look at the agreement again. It had now been well over a year since we had come to an agreement on the transition plan, and he was anxious to put the SA to rest. However, this time, I said that I wanted to have my own lawyer look over the agreement before I signed it, which led to one of the biggest disagreements we had ever had.

My dad's perspective was that we already had an agreement in place as to how the transition would work and that the SA was simply the fine print. But the SA also included details we had never taken into account or discussed, which is why I wanted to better understand it. I could have simply signed the SA and been done with it and, yes, that was an option I considered. But I was reluctant to sign something I didn't understand. Most of the clauses in the agreement were unclear to me. Acquiring my own legal advice on the matter made sense to me. And in fact there was a clause in the SA stating that all parties in the agreement should do exactly that.

My dad's experience with and trust in the support team likely gave him the confidence that the agreement was well-drafted and fair. Meanwhile, I felt it was important to understand the implications of the SA because I wanted to do well as my dad's successor. Part of that process was gaining as much knowledge as possible and that included reviewing the SA legally. The end result was that neither of us would sign the SA and that meant our transition plans were on the verge of imploding.

We didn't talk about the SA or the transition process for an entire year. Perhaps my dad took this breach in our relationship as a break in trust with me, and perhaps he even saw me as ungrateful for the opportunity to succeed him as the business owner and unaccepting of the terms to do so. That was not my interpretation nor my intention. During the making of the transition plan I did not make any demands or attempt to get more than I should. The terms were laid out and I accepted them. The primary issue I had with the SA was that it contained many rules, implications, and limitations that had never been discussed. If the SA had been presented earlier then the process would have gone more smoothly; but then perhaps I wouldn't be telling you this important tale of caution.

Two years after we had agreed on the transition plan terms, there was still no signed SA. As the line of communication between the two of us gradually reopened, I stuck to my idea of having my own legal counsel review the agreement. By this point, I was already running the business and had grown it to about twice the size that it had been at the time the deal was made, potentially doubling its value. The company had gone through a huge growth spurt in a short amount of time; revenues and efficiencies were up, and so were the profits. I wanted to make sure that my interests were considered in the SA as I had plans to grow the company even more. It was risky for me to go about it this way, I'll admit, and realistically my dad could have pulled out and made other plans, especially since the business was now worth twice as much.

My dad's resistance to my pursuit of legal advice diminished over the course of the year and he was now open to the idea. So, I hired my own lawyer to decipher the meaning of certain clauses in the agreement and clarify what it meant to be a shareholder. When I got my copy of the agreement back from my lawyer, it was filled with red ink and almost every page had a note on it. I focused on a handful of main clauses that I had specific issues with. My lawyer explained the various scenarios and outcomes of each clause and the risks I was exposed to. I took the seven points that were of main concern and asked him to rewrite the pertinent clauses so that they would balance the scales. He suggested that we directly contact my dad's lawyer to make the process smoother.

Wow, was that ever a big mistake.

First, I hadn't given my dad's lawyer notice that my lawyer would be contacting him. Second, and more importantly,

The Shareholders' Agreement

I had opened negotiations in such a way that each lawyer was now fighting for their client's best interests. My dad and I were caught in a legal situation while pretending nothing was going on. We would each consult with our respective lawyer who handled the situation on our behalves, and back and forth it went. We became extremely frustrated with each other and the whole process, and we ended up pushing the subject to the side for yet another year.

Once again, my ownership in the business, the work I had put in over the years, and my future were at risk. I admit it was my fault for opening up the discussion between the lawyers, but I was unaware that this would cause a greater issue. I had made a critical mistake and failed to see the root cause for why we were having so many difficulties getting the SA signed. I wasn't able to see that our business lawyer—also my dad's friend—had the best intentions in mind when composing the SA, but he had built in protections and clauses that were naturally in my dad's favour. The SA was written as such to allow my dad to be able to intervene in the business and rectify things as needed if I created major issues for the company while running it. The SA also contained clauses that would limit me and enable my dad to take control over the company at any point if necessary.

Fair enough, you say. But my point of view was that if I owned 99 percent of the stock in the business, my dad should not be able to outvote me and take back control of the company. If he were to do so at some point in the future, he would already have received the vast sum of the value and payouts that he was entitled to, and his "best interest" would now reflect a mere 1 percent of the value of the company. Had I left the SA as originally drafted, that would have been just one of the clauses that could have caused issues in the future.

It turned out that my dad had been led to believe that the agreement was much simpler and more straightforward than it was. Rather than trying to undermine my position in the company, he had simply trusted that his lawyer would look out for the company's best interest. My dad didn't know about the details in the SA highlighted by my lawyer. It became clear that he did not intend to include many of the restrictive clauses his lawyer had added into the document. He thought we were dealing with a boilerplate agreement.

After going through these negotiations with our lawyers and without a resolution in sight, we took yet another year away from resolving the SA disagreement. We both needed to step back for a moment and think about how we were going to approach the agreement the third time around. The good thing was that we had an understanding of what the other party was pushing for, what conditions they might be willing to accept, and what issues there would be no budging on.

Third Time's the Charm

Well over three years after the SA was first drafted, I decided to ease up on my approach. By this time I had made a new friend, a lawyer specializing in the restructuring and transitioning of companies. I decided to seek his help. Sure enough, he confirmed I had already done everything I shouldn't have done. After some consultation, I realized he could truly help me and I hired him officially. At this stage in the game I had come to grips with many of the clauses that I had wanted to change in earlier negotiating attempts. If I gave in a little, perhaps my dad and his lawyer would reciprocate. This tactic worked, and the interactions between us started to relax and even had an air of friendliness to them.

We chose to focus on the top three issues I had with the SA and see if we could craft an agreement that was fair to both parties. Before I addressed these issues with the core team, my new lawyer advised me to talk with my dad about these issues first and discuss why they were important to me, how they would affect us in the future, and so on. This approach eliminated any risk of my dad being caught off guard by my requests. It worked amazingly well, and we had several heart-to-heart conversations about the business and our future. It became clear that our intentions were in line with each other's despite how things seemed to be spelled out in the SA.

This time around it seemed like everything was coming together and we were close to making an agreement. We could both see the light at the end of the tunnel. A month or so after my dad and I had our talk, we arranged a meeting with our accounting team to openly discuss and note the current status of our transition. We were now all in agreement about the changes that needed to be made to the SA, and everyone involved breathed a sigh of relief. We walked out of that meeting happy and looking forward to moving on with our lives.

The final changes were made and we had the final version of the SA. By this point we had both almost forgotten what changes had even been made to the original document, so we had to review it all over again to make sure everything was in order. So my advice to you is this: when it's time for an agreement to be made, you need to act as soon as possible. Time is of the essence. Make it a priority to have the SA created, so you can review and sign it right away. I can't stress this enough. Even just waiting for this document to be prepared brought up the same frustration and negative outlook that had coloured our earlier discussions of the subject. Strike while the iron is hot, as they say.

I felt nervous when I opened my copy of the final SA as I was worried I would find mistakes or overlooked changes, and that these would cause even further delays. But everything was in order and a meeting was arranged to execute the agreement.

The big day had finally arrived! What was supposed to be an easy agreement to draft and sign had taken over three years and tens of thousands of dollars, and had caused almost irreparable damage. When we finally signed the SA, everyone shook hands, and my dad and I hugged. Everyone in the room smiled. We had finally done it.

Signing the Agreement

Conversations about the shareholders' agreement need to start at the same time as conversations about the transition plan. The actual transition phase, when shares and ownership are transferred, should not begin until the SA is signed. This ensures that everyone understands the terms. If there is resistance at this point it puts added pressure on the successor and may make both parties reconsider whether it is the right choice for the successor to take over the business. I had issues with the SA because it was presented to me after I had already grown the business and increased its value under a different set of assumptions. The SA changed the meaning of the deal. So, my recommendation is to draw up the SA as part of the agreement for the transition plan and at the same time.

Here are some other recommendations to consider when drafting an SA:

- Ensure that a member of your core team, ideally whoever you most often meet with (in our case, our accountant), takes meeting notes on everything that is discussed. This can help immensely with discussions down the road. If there are any disagreements or people forget about decisions that were made or items that were previously discussed, you can refer to the meeting notes.
- Understand that there will be some give and take. It's not always best to have the SA be drafted for the benefit of one side only. As the exiting owner, remember that your successor should be looking out for their interests, as decisions made today will have an impact for many years in the future. As the successor, be mindful that the business owner likely wants to preserve and ensure their legacy and the success of the company.

- Review the SA with a lawyer. Both parties, the exiting owner and the successor, should be aware of what the SA asks of each of them. Consider removing or modifying clauses that do not reflect your unique situation to reduce possible conflict.
- Resolve disagreements as soon as possible. If possible, the exiting owner and the successor should have direct conversations about any issues and try to reach an agreement before taking them to a lawyer.
- Use the transition team to help mediate disagreements as much as possible. It helps to hear things from someone else's perspective other than your family's or partner's.
- Support the right to outside counsel if either party chooses to consult another lawyer. However, the core team should be involved to ensure that the outside lawyer(s) has a clear view and understanding of the transition and the desired end result. This will avoid either party from narrating their own version of the story to their lawyer and affecting how their lawyer approaches the SA. I did not involve the core team in my legal vetting process of the SA. This led to skewed results and legal advice that ultimately led to conflict and misunderstanding.

In the end, the exiting owner is the key person to take charge of the entire transition process. It's your family business after all. Keep the pressure on your transition team to get things done in a timely manner. Any changes, edits, or agreements that have been made in the SA or the transition deal should be documented and implemented immediately. This can be the difference between a smooth process or one fraught with difficulty.

CHAPTER 8

Making the Deal

MAKING THE DEAL comes after a transition plan is in place and a shareholder's agreement is drafted up and ready to go. At this point, the exiting owner and their successor can begin formalizing the process of transitioning business ownership.

The main point here is that it is one thing to have a transition plan in place and a shareholders' agreement ready, and another thing entirely to have both the successor and exiting owner on the same page and working together on it. For the exiting owner, the essence of making the deal is to get the successor's buy-in and participation in the proposed transition plan. You want them to see the opportunity available to them.

Our Transition Plan

The general idea behind our deal was that my dad was offering me the opportunity to take over the leadership and ownership of the business and, in exchange, I would provide him with the means to step away from the business and take retirement. The plan answered the questions of how this transition process would work, and how the buyout would unfold over the years to come. To make the plan succeed, we both had to fulfil our own ends of the deal.

By this point, I had already graduated college and had put in two solid years of work at the company, which made it clear that I was serious about my intentions to take over the business. Looking back at it now, I suppose that this is what my dad wanted to see from me: commitment and dedication to the business. It gave him the confidence to move forward with the transition process and so he contacted our accountant and told him we were ready to put a transition plan together.

I did not have much involvement in the actual discussions and meetings regarding the creation of the transition plan. It was a plan already in the works before it was presented to me. When my dad and I went to our first meeting to discuss the plan and how it would all work, our transition team presented a "wasting freeze," an arrangement in which a value would be placed on the business and the value of the shares would be frozen, at which point my dad could redeem a percentage of these frozen shares every year for a period of ten years.

This was a great approach for transitioning the business because I had no means of paying for the business at this point in time. According to our plan, the business would buy out the shares from my dad through its earnings. This would give him the retirement income that he needed for the next ten years, and it would allow me and the business the time to pay off that income while also providing some tax-planning opportunities.

Our team further explained that although the value of the shares that my dad owned (preferred shares) would be frozen from the set date, the shares I owned (common shares) would be tied to the future growth and value of the business. That meant that if I could grow the company, and its value went up, I would be entitled to the new value, less what was owed on the outstanding preferred shares that my dad owned. This gave me the incentive to do my best to grow the company and create additional funds to buy out my dad quicker. Not to mention that any increase in the value of the company would be to my benefit.

Wow, I liked this idea! All I could see was the opportunity. Sure, ten years sounded like a long time, but since I had no capital, this was the next best thing. I highly recommend putting some form of freeze or even a partial freeze on your own transition plan as it will boost motivation and buy-in from your successor.

One point of contention that can crop up in this scenario is the placing of a value on the business. As I mentioned earlier, some family business owners can be sensitive about the value of their businesses. When they try to put a number on it, especially if that number directly correlates to how much retirement income they may receive, they may overinflate the value. I realized that the lower the valuation on the business, the better it would be for me as the amount to be paid off would be less. But I didn't push for a lower valuation out of respect for my dad. For the most part the valuation of the business was influenced by my dad's retirement needs.

We came to an agreement on the business's value and then included an employment salary for my dad, which added further value for him. The total value of the deal was an amount that was a little more than what the business was worth, but it was an amount that was able to provide my dad with a comfortable retirement.

To give you an example of how an exiting owner might calculate their retirement income, let's consider that you want to receive $100,000 per year over ten years to fund your retirement lifestyle, but your business is only worth $750,000. This amount will only provide you with seven and a half years of income at that rate. If you want the funds to last all ten years, then you will need to either come up with an extra $250,000 or scale your yearly income back to $75,000 per year for ten years.

This reflects the situation we encountered: the total value of the business at the time of transition was less than what my dad wanted for retirement. So we included an employment agreement, which would keep him on the company's payroll and make up that extra value he wanted. Going back to the example above, you could build in an employment agreement worth $250,000 in addition to the $750,000 business valuation, giving you a total of $1,000,000 in value.

Adding in an employment agreement to the deal was a scenario that worked out well for us. During the first few years of the transition my dad would still be involved with the business as he gradually evolved into a consulting/coaching role and therefore was entitled to a salary for his services. My dad's financial planner then arranged for a portion of the money received to fund his everyday living expenses, and another portion went toward his investment plans to further fund retirement.

Now, obviously you can spread the money out over a longer period of time; this will depend on both the total value of the deal and the desired retirement income. The above is just an example of how we approached our deal.

When composing the deal, make sure that everyone—the business owner, the successor, and the transition team—is aware of the total value of the deal, inclusive of business value, additional employment salary, and any other benefits or perks that have monetary value. As in many family businesses, the family's and owner's lifestyles can be in part funded by expensing relevant costs such as cars, lunches, cell phones, and so forth, to the business. These are all costs that should be taken into account when arriving at the value of the deal in order to avoid confusion or misunderstandings. For instance, if the total value of the deal is $1,000,000, then it must be clear what that amount represents. Does it exclude other perks and values that come with employment, or is it inclusive of any and all value that the exiting owner is to receive?

In our previous example, we established a $250,000 employment value that included a salary and any other ancillary expenses required to undertake work for the company. In essence, my dad was to receive up to $250,000 in employment value regardless of whether it was paid out through a salary or through other benefits and perks. We were able to anticipate how much value my dad would extract in the form of company perks like vehicles, cell phones, entertainment (dinners, golf, sporting events, etc.), and so on. The yearly total of those amounts was taken into account and included the deal's total value.

Realizing the total value of the deal may be a reality check as to how the exiting owner may need to adjust lifestyle and spending as they move forward into retirement. They will now know how much money they can expect through the transition process.

When it comes to extracting value from the business, the exiting owner should avoid pulling out all the available cash. Be aware of the health of the business and enable its ability to keep up with the payment schedule set out in the agreement. This is something that my dad and I discussed in passing; we decided that we would adjust the payout amounts depending on how the business was doing at any given point in time. Our plan would function as a guide, and we would follow it as closely as we could, but he allowed for some flexibility because we didn't know where we would be in the years ahead, and he did not want to put extra pressure on me or the business. We included a clause in the shareholders' agreement that gave us that flexibility.

For the first year of the transition, we stuck to the set amounts outlined by the plan, but by the second year, the company was doing much better financially. We decided to accelerate the payout amounts so that by the fifth year of the ten-year plan, about 70 percent of the value of the deal would have already been redeemed. This would allow my dad to further plan for and invest those funds, but more importantly it would reduce the risk of anything happening to his nest egg. If the business were to get into trouble at some point during the ten-year timeline then those funds could be at risk, and if the business were to go bankrupt then he would lose it all. To reduce the possibility of that happening, we wanted to redeem the value of his preferred shares as quickly as was reasonable for the business.

This was how our transition plan would work. However, the process of getting through the transitioning years is another story. Regardless of what your family business's transition plan may be, the most important guidelines to follow are to be clear about the plan's intentions and to ensure all parties involved have a general understanding of how the process is going to work. From there, you can work together toward the same goal of ensuring transition success.

> **All parties should understand how the process will pan out.**

The Implementation Phase: Key Points

The implementation phase is a plan of attack for the transition of ownership and seeing it through to execution. It involves four key steps:

- Creating a transition plan
- Assembling a transition team
- Drafting a shareholders' agreement
- Making the deal

Once you have completed the priming phase and are ready to take the next step in transitioning ownership, the first task is to inform your accountant or lawyer that you want to move forward with the creation of a transition plan. When the plan is drafted, you'll need to assemble your transition team. This is the group of professionals who will be helping you through the transition process as outlined in the plan. The details of how the plan will unfold will dictate which team members you need to include, such as a consultant, a financial planner, a business banker, and so forth.

With your transition plan and team in place, the third step is to have your lawyer prepare a shareholders' agreement (SA). This is an agreement that will be signed by both the exiting owner and the successor. The SA covers the rules and guidelines as to how the transition is to be executed as well as the shareholders' roles and expectations. The final step in the process is to make the deal with your successor. This is the process of formally presenting the transition plan and SA to the successor, attaining their support and buy-in to the plan, signing off on the agreement, and beginning the transition of ownership.

PART THREE

E is for Ensuring Success

Ensuring success is the final stage in the journey of transitioning the family business. By this point, you have a transition plan that has been created for your unique situation, the plan has been implemented or is about to be, and business ownership is ready to begin transferring from one generation to the next.

Remember that the actual plan for how to transition ownership of the business is only part of the succession equation. As in any plan, action is required to achieve the desired goal. During this period, the focus is on maintaining healthy and harmonious family relationships as the shift in power and responsibilities becomes more apparent.

Since this process can take many years to complete, both the successor and the exiting owner will need to maintain focus so that the transition stays on target. The ensuring success phase focuses on, well, exactly that: ensuring that everything goes as smoothly as possible in order to achieve succession.

During the transitioning years, the successor will naturally begin taking on more of the leadership role in the business and will need continued support and mentoring from the exiting owner. As the successor exhibits their ability to lead, the exiting owner must also understand their new role, which is to let go. After a detachment process that allows for a graceful exit from the business, the exiting owner finally hands the reins to the successor, resulting in a transition of power not only in the business but perhaps also within the family itself.

Dealing with and avoiding conflict between those involvedwill be a top priority, because at the end of the day, what's the point of transitioning the family business if family relations fall apart in the process?

CHAPTER 9

Supporting the Successor

As the transition of ownership begins, the exiting owner should ensure that the successor is ready to handle the responsibilities of business ownership. The same concepts that apply to the grooming of the successor during the priming phase continue to be relevant well into the transition of ownership stage. It is essential to keep coaching the successor until they are capable of running the business on their own. Only once that is achieved will the exiting owner likely feel comfortable letting go of the business. And even once the exiting owner has successfully transitioned their business, it will still be worthwhile for them to serve as a coach and mentor to their successor.

By this stage in the transition journey, everyone understands that the successor is to become the leader of the business, and that the exiting owner will soon step down from the position. But for a moment imagine being in your successor's shoes: You are the child of the owner, set to inherit the throne. Everyone—your family, friends, coworkers, clients—has expectations for what you are to achieve. What are you thinking? How are you handling the pressure? Do you doubt your ability to take over and lead the business? What kind of support or help might you need to ensure that you deliver? These are just a few thoughts that may run, as they did with me, through the mind of a successor.

> **Coach the successor until you feel they are ready to run the business.**

In my experience there are a few specific factors that can hinder a successor's performance and ability to lead. If not addressed these issues may lead to a slowdown or even a plateau in the successor's confidence, motivation, and overall progression. If and when this happens, finding solutions will be a challenge if the exiting owner doesn't understand the problems the successor is experiencing. Some of the factors that may affect the successor include:

- Inexperience
- The high expectations of the exiting owner
- Feelings of entitlement
- Lifestyle differences

By making the attempt to better understand your successor's situation you can gain some insight into how you can aid their development in becoming a capable leader of the business.

Inexperience

There are two forms of inexperience that may apply in this situation: One is a lack of the technical knowledge and the skill sets required for the business in question, and the other is a lack of general business experience, or simply not knowing how to think like a business owner. In my case, my lack of experience was in the trade property restoration. For me to be successful and confident in my dealings, I needed to have sufficient experience in the industry.

Imagine trying to run a business when you have little experience and knowledge of the service or product the company delivers. That's not the best recipe for success. Therefore, during the priming phase I learned the "hands-on" aspects of the business from the ground up, and I continued my industry certification process, leading me to attain a master restorer designation. After ten years of being involved in the business, I finally had all the experience and knowledge I needed to excel, not to mention the added confidence of knowing that I was one of just a few working in my area who had this designation.

The second type of inexperience relates to *running* a business. Knowing how to address the many facets of business management requires a different set of skills, from negotiating a new banking deal to handling legal issues, clients, vendors, and suppliers, from managing cash flow to hiring and dismissing staff. This is why it's essential to train your successor to effectively run the business. Laying this groundwork will both enable you to retire without worry and allow the company to keep functioning after the successor has taken over.

Having the successor shadow you during day-to-day business activities is the best way to teach them the skills required. As your successor's confidence and ability to handle business dealings grow, you should be offloading more responsibility and letting them handle tasks independently. This is the fastest way for a successor to learn how to problem-solve—by tackling challenges and obstacles on their own. The size of a problem is not the issue; what matters is the size of the person. By this I mean that the bigger you are as a person, in terms of experience and abilities, the better you will be able to handle any situation—a requirement for the makings of a great leader.

I recommend that successors join business networking groups and industry associations. There are many benefits to making connections across different business fields and gaining experience in public speaking. They include marketing opportunities and prospective leads as well as the potential to maximize learning in the shortest amount of time. But the most important benefit I discovered when I joined networking groups was meeting other leaders in situations similar to my own. There is nothing more empowering and motivating than discovering other people who share the same issues and concerns as you. And if the opportunity arises where you meet somebody who is a few years ahead of you in the succession process, then this relationship can serve as a great support system through your own journey.

At these networking meetings, I discovered that my

dad and I had made it quite far together; we had worked through many of the issues that can stall or even inhibit succession. I found myself sharing my own ideas and experiences with other soon-to-be owners, which also helped me conceptualize and realize what I had learned and how it could help others.

Within these new social circles, I met successful business leaders and owners who had businesses much bigger than mine, many of whom would become my friends and mentors. They became people that I could bounce ideas off and learn from. Tapping into this knowledge base enhanced my business IQ and saved me years of trial and error. Having somebody outside your family business share their business knowledge is important and refreshing. Their advice may be more objective and potentially more valid, as it won't be influenced by any personal biases that can result from the parent-child relationship.

Surrounding yourself with successful achievers can be a sobering and humbling experience; it can keep an overly active ego in check while encouraging the successor to reach for higher goals.

High Expectations

A parent's expectations for their child/successor can feel like a heavy burden for the successor. Even worse, it can have a paralyzing effect on the successor, especially if they are young and feel unsupported. A seasoned business owner is equipped to handle the pressures of the business world. They know how to set goals and push forward to achieve them. As the exiting owner, you are able to see the goal of your child succeeding in the business. Your successor, however, may not see the goal as clearly, and they may become overwhelmed with the process of getting there. Breaking up the steps in the transition process into smaller, more easily attainable goals can ease everyone's anxieties.

My advice is for the exiting owner and the successor to meet frequently and discuss the expectations associated with accomplishing each goal. Assign realistic expectations and allow the successor to take responsibility for the tasks set out for them. Place the successor in situations where they are able to take the credit when things go right and the blame when they don't. Assess their progression and provide constructive feedback—both positive and negative—throughout the process. Help the successor set new annual goals, increasing their level of responsibility and productivity for each successive year.

During our transition, the idea of taking over the business was the ultimate goal in my mind. I didn't take much time to celebrate or be content with the progress I was making. Instead I had a notion that I should only allow myself to be happy when I finally took over the business. I was the main culprit when it came to placing pressure on myself. Instead, I should have taken the time to realize how well the process was going. From taking over the accounting department to growing business revenue to becoming the general manager, I got caught up in the grind to clearly see what we had achieved. Successors should be encouraged to acknowledge their accomplishments to relieve some of the pressure of expectations.

The company staff will also have their own expectations. These expectations may pose a different challenge for the successor than parental ones. The successor may feel that they are auditioning for the chance to earn trust and respect among employees and management. Thanks to my dad's effective priming techniques, I developed the right work ethic throughout my upbringing, which helped me earn our staff's respect. After I graduated from high school my involvement in the business began to increase, and so did the rumours among the staff that I would take over the business one day.

I remember a time in particular when I went to a jobsite with one of our senior employees to do some quality assurance. On the drive there, we discussed the cars we liked and the types of cars we owned. It came up in conversation that I had bought my own car; the senior employee was quite surprised as he had assumed that my dad had bought it for me. I explained that I had worked for three years every day after school at the local golf course, washing golf carts to save enough money to buy the car. My sense of this is that it demonstrated to him—and, by extension, the rest of the staff—that I was not afraid to work toward a goal and that I was not about to be given anything for free.

I realized that I would need to show our business's employees that I wasn't afraid of hard work in order to gain the respect of those I planned to lead one day. I continued working alongside that senior employee, performing every task he asked. He never held back or treated me differently, nor did I expect him to. He was well regarded within the company, and being able to earn his respect made a difference in how I was perceived. If the staff does not respect the leader-to-be, they can become resentful, making it an uphill battle for the successor to gain their full support in the future. Worse yet, the staff may leave the company altogether.

As the leader of your company, it is important to do what you can to promote and support a good work ethic in your successor and fulfill the expectations of the staff. Avoid favortism and leniency in the workplace by treating your successor as you would others. Remember, you have already done most of the heavy lifting for this process in the priming phase. Remind yourself that as your successor moves up in rank and assumes more responsibility, they must demonstrate that they have what it takes to succeed and will not shy away from challenges that present themselves.

Entitlement

Some successors assume a certain attitude because of their position in the company and that tends to come out in their dealings with employees and with the company as a whole. This sense of entitlement was something I was guilty of myself. Though I would like to think that I never adopted an air of superiority, the reality is that there were moments I'm not proud of—moments when I should have checked my ego at the door. Occasionally I dismissed feedback and advice from senior employees, and I sometimes believed that company policies didn't always apply to me. Successors need to understand that their actions and demeanours are magnified by their roles within the company, and they carry an increased significance for everyone involved.

A successor must earn the respect of seasoned staff.

Most businesses will have staff who have been with the company for a long time and who are loyal to the exiting owner's leadership. The successor needs to learn how to lead people older than themselves, as these employees may harbour thoughts like "What does this kid know about the business?" and "They've probably never worked a full day in their life." The successor needs to respect the experience of seasoned staff, understand that they have much to learn from their senior employees, and be willing to earn their respect.

As I mentioned previously, a large part of earning staff's trust and respect is being willing to put in the work required at the ground level without expecting preferential treatment. When I moved from working in the field to working in the office, I was required to be at work by 8 a.m., the same time as the rest of the staff. Things began to slip, and I would roll in some time around 9 a.m., under the assumption that I could get away with it. The office staff began making remarks and jokes about how I always came in late. I brought this up with my dad and told him I was annoyed with their reaction to the hours I kept and that I wanted to put them in their place. He nipped that idea in the bud right away and set me straight: He didn't support my outlook on relaxed work hours, and he suggested that I follow the company policy. This is just one example of how a successor's ego might get in their own way. When it does, it's important for both the successor and the exiting owner to identify and rectify it.

As the successor begins to learn more about the business world, they might begin to develop a superior attitude, and with it a larger ego to keep in check. During my college years, I would learn something new every day in my business classes. When I would come into work the next day and see that our business was not following the practices that I had learned about in school, I would ask questions like "What do you mean we don't have a SWOT analysis?" or "We don't have a system for evaluating employee performance?" While I will say that what I was learning was indeed valid and did have value that the company could benefit from, I was not taking into account how a business realistically ran, not to mention the culture of this particular business—or the fact that there is a time and a place for everything.

Just because my dad didn't have a business degree didn't mean he didn't understand what I was trying to do. He actually understood it quite well, but he also knew the business well enough to know that performing a SWOT analysis was not a top priority at that point in time. It is important for a successor to understand the current business culture before attempting to change it.

As a final note with respect to taming the successor's ego, expect that a younger person will naturally be a bit brash and full of energy, and sometimes they will exhibit an off-putting attitude. Try to cut them a little slack—after all, you want that energy to fuel the company's future success. Be aware of their blind spots, however; many younger people have not yet gained wisdom through experience. Reinforcing company policies and holding the successor to the same expectations as others will help them see where they stand.

For the successor, the time to enjoy the perks and benefits of business ownership will come, but only once they understand that a leader leads by example, earns respect, and focuses on results and not efforts.

Lifestyle Differences

The demands, responsibilities, and expectations of business ownership can take a toll on the successor and result in an imbalance between their work life and their personal life. If this imbalance is not addressed early on, it can cause further issues, not just for the succession progress, but also for the relationship between the exiting owner and the successor, and for the successor's emotional state.

Of course, lifestyle factors can vary greatly depending on the age of the successor and their stage in life, their goals, their focus, and their interests. A successor who is already in their thirties or forties may be more settled down than someone still in their twenties, and they likely have a better grasp on how to achieve the balance they desire. It is also true that with younger successors, conflicts between the demands of their peer group and the demands of their business will more likely occur. This will especially be the case if the successor is the only one in their peer group (and they probably are) who is taking over a family business. Their friends are unlikely to understand what the successor is going through, and if the successor holds that peer group in high regard, then they may be strongly influenced by their interests rather than the business's best interests. When this happens, the successor's point of reference shifts to a place outside of the business, and they may want to take time off to travel, hang out at the beach, or meet their friends to play volleyball on Friday afternoons. Of course, all of these interests are fine given the right circumstances, but if your successor's attachment to their peer group begins to eclipse their work ethic or interest in the business then it is something that needs to be monitored so it does not get out of hand.

After high school some of my friends took a year off to travel. I struggled with this as I watched them enjoy their newfound freedom because I wanted to be part of that experience. But I also knew it would set back my progress with the business and so, with much encouragement from my parents, I continued to work in the family business and went to college as planned.

Even in college, I continued to find myself with a unique set of responsibilities and expectations that my new peer groups did not seem to have. On the one hand I was a young student and naturally wanted to partake in everything that came with that lifestyle, but on the other hand I was being groomed to take over the business and had to act accordingly. Sometimes I struggled with the expectations from both sides. At times, I just wanted to be a kid for once, to do what kids my age were doing without a care in the world. But that feeling subsides when you realize the opportunity that is in front of you. Some sacrifices need to be made in order to reach your goals. And the goal I had was taking over my family business before I was thirty and being able to provide my dad with a comfortable retirement. Do I regret putting in the effort required? Not for a minute.

This is not to say that I didn't take time for myself along the way. Heck, I still travelled, relaxed at the beach during the summer, and went to more parties than I can remember—but I knew where my focus should be and that was on my studies, the business, and my role within it.

As I got older I thought more about my future. I realized that I needed to surround myself with people who shared a similar mindset—people I could learn from, and who would ultimately support my vision of where I wanted to go. I had already experienced the opposite effect in college, when my friends' interests had had a big hand in shaping my own. If all your friends are going to a party, then guess what? Chances are you will too. I knew, then, that the same must also be true when it comes to more productive tasks.

When I surrounded myself with like-minded people, the battle of opposing interests—the search for balance between my personal and business lives—began to fade. My new peer group, social outings, and interests took over my business life, and my business life became my personal life. I no longer had this duality of worlds, each pulling me away from the other; instead they were now both working together toward my goals.

This is something that happens to every successful

business owner. At some point or another, we make a decision about which influences we allow to shape and impact our lives. As the successor matures, their interests and ambitions will become clearer, allowing them to find the path required to achieve their goals and their desired lifestyle. But until then, the challenge for the successor during their younger years is to avoid being overly influenced by a peer group, which can divert or slow down the progression of the succession plan.

If the time and effort is put into priming the successor, then you, as the exiting owner, have likely instilled the right values and outlook in your successor. As a parent and business owner, you will need to understand that your child and successor will have other interests at any given point in time. Allow them the flexibility to explore these interests. It's important that the successor find the right balance between their business and personal lives as too much freedom can cause them to lose focus and too much work can lead to them burning out or developing feelings of resentment or regret.

CHAPTER 10

Letting Go

ULTIMATELY, for a successful transition to be accomplished, the exiting owner must allow their successor to take on more responsibilities. This is a process that requires practice and effort on the part of the exiting owner—it is not always an easy thing to let someone else take the driver's seat, to let go of the business that you created and the power that comes with it. But with awareness and the right approach, it can be a rewarding process. The reward of course is being able to transfer responsibilities to a capable successor, knowing that your business is in good hands, so you can focus on more important things—like improving your golf game.

I witnessed my dad go through this process and I saw how he coped with the change. It was evident that he was committed to succession—he wanted to see the business survive into its second generation and he wanted to provide me with a bright future while providing himself with the security he ultimately needed.

During this stage the exiting owner needs to focus more on ensuring succession and less on ensuring business success. It is now time for them to step away from the business and let the new leader operate in their new role. If they have done an effective job of grooming the successor for leadership, they can be confident that their business will be in good hands.

The process of letting go may be accomplished in many ways, some not as effective as others. Certain methods can stall or even derail transition plans. One common trajectory is that the exiting owner is able to let go initially, but eventually or periodically returns to the business to "check in" on their successor. Another scenario is that the exiting owner lets go of their former role at such a slow pace that it prolongs the transition process. These are the two worst ways in which an exiting owner can behave. Having two different leaders can negatively impact a business. It creates a tense working relationship between an exiting owner and their successor, causing frustration and confusion for everybody involved.

What would cause an exiting owner to feel like they have to behave in this way? There are three determining factors that may hinder a business owner from letting go:

1. Fear of letting the successor lead
2. Trepidation about life outside of the business
3. Anxiety about the state of present and future finances

Understandably, the exiting owner may have trouble letting go if there is doubt in their mind about their successor's ability to lead the business. But by this point in time, they should have already spent many years working alongside and grooming their successors as they deemed fit. In any transition, there comes a time when the successor will be as ready as they can be, and they must be allowed to take the plunge.

The exiting owner's personal life may also factor into the equation, particularly if they do not have an identity outside of the business or don't have any plans for their newfound freedom. Without hobbies or travel plans in which they can invest their time, an exiting owner will find it harder to let go of their business.

Finally, if the exiting owner's finances are not in line with their retirement plans, it will be more difficult for them to step away completely. It can be tempting for an exiting owner to hold onto the business as a source of income security.

Believe it or not, all three of these factors are under an exiting owner's control. If you find yourself in a position where you are unable to let go of the business, you need to take a look and identify which of these factors may be holding you back. You do not want to become the bottleneck in the succession process. A big part of learning to let go is being able to identify when your successor is ready to lead, and when that time comes, you will need to step to the side and see how your successor does. There is of course going to be a trial-and-error phase—mistakes will happen and challenges will arise—but just as you did when you were starting out, your successor will have to learn by doing.

In our own transition situation, I believe all three aspects were well taken care of. After years of mentorship and guidance, my dad was comfortable with my ability to lead the company, and so he began letting go slowly, allowing me to take on more responsibility over time until he didn't have as much to do in the business.

As soon as he felt fully comfortable letting me run the business, my dad took off for an extended holiday to Mexico and caught up on some much-needed R&R. When he got back, he was elected president of the local Rotary Club and he got more involved in philanthropic activities. In terms of finances, he had to get used to living on a set income as outlined by the transition plan. He struggled initially but as time went on he developed new spending habits, and he learned to live without tapping in to the business for additional funds. Although it took some time, work, and patience from both of us, he was able to let go in a gracious manner, in a way that not only made him feel comfortable but also did not hinder my ability to lead.

Who's the Boss Now?

At some point during a family business transition—which could be in year one or year nine—you will realize that your responsibilities will have decreased to the point that your role within the company has completely changed. At this point, it's time to ask yourself that key question: "Who's the boss now?"

This question is important as it will help owners and successors alike find the answers needed for a smooth transition. Thinking about the answer to the question will help you come to grips with the reality of the transition process. The company leader is not necessarily the person who owns the most stock in the business; rather, it is the person who sets the pace, leads by example, and ultimately sees themself as the leader regardless of what may be true on paper. Eventually the exiting owner will arrive at a point when their successor now handles these tasks and is for the most part running the company—the point when the management, staff, and perhaps even they see the successor as the leader of the company.

> A successful company leader sets the pace and leads by example.

Remember that up until this point, the exiting owner is still in control of the transition and needs to do what is best for the business and its progression. So when the moment comes that you feel comfortable that the answer to "who's the boss now?" is your successor, then you know it is time to step aside. When the time has finally come that you can sleep comfortably at night knowing that the company is in your successor's capable hands, that's the time to make it official.

For my dad and me, that moment came when I was in my late twenties. By that time I had already been running the show for several years and had earned the staff's trust as someone who could lead the business. We had a company-wide staff meeting and my dad appointed me as the general manager of the company: a clear show of trust and a stamp of approval that others could count on.

The New Leader

In my opinion the most important attribute for the successor is the confidence to see themself as the owner of the business whether they own any shares or not. Every action and decision they make must be viewed through an owner's lens, putting the business's best interests first. This demonstrates an understanding that maintaining the business in a healthy and secure state is the key to stability and longevity. The successor understands that the decisions they make impact not just themself but other family members, shareholders, staff, suppliers, and so forth.

Developing an Ownership Mentality

The development of an ownership mentality begins early in the successor's life, during the priming phase, and progresses through the transition period and continues once the succession has been completed. Basic actions like sweeping the front entrance to the office and picking up a discarded candy wrapper from the hallway floor without waiting for someone else to do it provides some evidence of this mentality. More profound examples include voluntarily taking a pay cut and not accepting a bonus when the company is in a bad financial spot, and assuming more responsibility by picking up slack in overburdened departments.

From an early age I felt I had to hold myself and my actions to a high standard. When I was a teenager working in the family business, I couldn't conceptualize or understand what business ownership really meant, nor what the attributes of a great successor were. However I did know that I needed to respect the business, and ensure that others did too. It was important to uphold policies and decisions made by my dad and to support how he wanted the business to run. I knew that keeping a tidy uniform, a clean vehicle, and a professional demeanour was a critical part of how the company would be perceived by our clients, our people, and the public. For me this was about taking pride in and supporting a business that reflected on me and our family as a whole.

As my involvement in the business increased, so did my owner-like actions. After I graduated from college I jumped into the business headfirst by working hard to put the business on a healthier plan. At that time the business was turning a small profit but not enough to fund expansion plans, give out raises, or weather a downturn.

A year after I graduated, our head accountant/bookkeeper left the company, creating an opening for a crucial position within the company. I volunteered for the position, knowing that I could save the company a salary while at the same time learning that end of the business. Sure enough, I was able to learn a whole other side of the business: revenues, costs, efficiencies, margins, you name it.

For over a year I handled all the accounting and bookkeeping for the company while also performing all my other managerial duties. I worked long hours and almost every weekend, during which I did not earn any extra pay. By the end of it, the company had saved the cost of two extra salaries, tightened up on expenditures, and became more efficient. The proof was in the pudding: Profits were way up.

Only once we had achieved the results we needed was I able to take a step back and realize that I could not keep at this pace forever. I looked at my desk where I had stacked multiple empty energy drink bottles and coffee cups. That was the moment when I decided to replace myself in the accounting department, so I could free myself to work on other areas of the business.

Through this process I don't remember my dad saying anything to me about how we should deal with the vacancy in accounting. He never once said that I should take over that position or that I should work crazy hours and weekends for an entire year. I saw the opening and understood that I could benefit from taking over the job and that the business would benefit from my involvement. I think my dad wanted to see if I could handle the challenge.

A successful transition depends on the initiative and determination of the successor to act in the best interests of the business. Even now, when it comes to the business I put myself in the mindset of a parent nurturing a child. Everything takes second place to caring for the child. I feel that this is what it takes to develop a great business and to become a successful businessman: a no excuses, get it done type of mentality. A great successor understands that business ownership is a privilege and an opportunity not to be taken for granted. Ownership is not a birthright. The successor should demonstrate gratitude for the opportunity and strive to add value to the business. They should continue to educate themself about the industry and business ownership.

In the early stages in our transition my dad and I actually had several sit-downs regarding the opportunity in front of me. At times I wasn't really sure where I was heading, and it wasn't clear that I appreciated my situation. However, my appreciation became much clearer as I matured. As a first-generation owner, be aware that this will usually be the case and temper your expectations—a successor's outlook at age thirty-two will be much different than at age twenty-two.

Nonetheless, you should keep an eye out for signs of entitlement or poor performance in your successor. Set clear expectations, and establish a progression path. By establishing benchmarks for performance, you can monitor their progress. If your child is ambitious, puts in effort to bring value to the business, and strives for more, then you are both on the right track. If, however, your successor doesn't reach beyond middle management and their performance stagnates while they patiently wait for a promotion, then you will need to determine their motivations and re-evaluate your approach to transition. You need to make the decisions that are best for the business, and if your child is simply not up to the task of taking on a senior role, you will have to have a serious conversation with them. They will need to either step up to the

> A successor must understand that business ownership is a great opportunity.

task or step aside until they're prepared to demonstrate that they are ready.

Besides working hard, I read extensively, focusing on books that would enhance my business knowledge. I delved into accounting, sales, marketing, operations, and finance management in order to develop the mindset of a business owner. After my stint in the accounting department, I spent two years in sales and marketing as the company was now ready to take on more clients. I wanted to make my own mark on the business and to demonstrate my worth to the enterprise. I brought in new clients and, along with them, new revenue. In those two years I more than doubled business revenue, developed a loyal client base, and further gained the respect of my dad, our staff, and our clients.

Obviously, these attributes aren't a make-it or break-it kind of deal. Don't panic if these qualities don't emerge from your successor right away; it can take years to develop the awareness needed to be a good business leader. Personally, I didn't make the effort until I was in my mid-twenties, and frankly before then, I was quite a different person. My performance was acceptable but not great, and certainly not at the level required to take over a business. My dad stuck with me, though, constantly coaching and mentoring me, knowing I would one day exhibit the signs of a great successor. I am thankful for that.

CHAPTER 11

Managing Conflict

For the exiting owner, with a capable successor in their corner, succession is in sight and fast approaching. All there is left for each of you to do is hold up your end of the bargain and make it through the remaining transitioning years. But during this time challenges can still arise. Your ability to overcome them as partners will be crucial for transition success.

I was originally going to call this section "avoiding conflict" but I don't think there is any way to achieve that. Undoubtedly, there will always be some conflict that will arise between family members, let alone those who work in the same business. That said, there are ways to reduce the frequency of conflict that may appear between the exiting owner and the successor:

- Pick a lane and stay in it
- Honour your agreements

- Ensure clarity
- Exhibit professional conduct
- Foster mutual respect
- Rely on your transition team
- Communicate through planned meetings

Both parties must acknowledge that disagreements will happen over the years. These could be over subjects such as the direction of the company, business strategy, and even small details like where the next holiday party should be held.

Conflict is part of any relationship, whether it be with friends, family, or business partners; we can't control this. What we can control is how we handle it, how we learn to avoid it, and how we move past it.

Pick a Lane and Stay In It

Once an exiting owner gives responsibility to their successor, they should respect the successor's subsequent decisions on related matters. Avoid micromanaging, nitpicking, and second-guessing a successor's decisions. This is one of the most frustrating and annoying things that a successor can encounter, and it can take the wind out of their sails. If you have to interfere or comment, it should be because you see immediate danger to the business, or you believe your feedback can truly benefit the successor in their future actions.

As the transition continues and the successor exhibits their ability to run the business, the exiting owner's role should gradually diminish. Once the exit has finally taken place, it should stay that way. The exiting owner should avoid returning periodically to check emails, make calls, and review the books. The business needs to operate without the previous owner's involvement in order to adapt to the new leader. The continued presence of an owner can create conflicting perceptions of authority among the staff. As the new leader establishes themself, the previous leader should also be seen to respect their position.

When my dad learned to let go of running the business, he had no problem being away from the business for weeks, even months at a time, but there were moments when he simply forgot that he was no longer the boss. In one instance, he wanted some yard work done at his house, and so he called the office, talked to our coordinator, and arranged for one of our staff to help him with the work. There were other appointments and customers, but instead, one of our newer employees went to help my dad for the day. You can see how this kind of behaviour might undermine the chain of command and negatively impact the business. Of course, I'm always going to help my dad in any way I can, but there is a better way to do it—a way that doesn't cause conflict.

For both the exiting leader and the successor, getting on the same page is a learning process. Eventually my dad limited his dealings in the business to the point that he would ask me directly when he needed something in order to eliminate confusion and get the desired results.

Honour Your Agreements

Limiting or altogether avoiding making changes to the

original deal will greatly reduce any chances of conflict between the exiting owner and their successor. The deal that you have both agreed to in the transition plan and shareholders' agreement should remain intact for the most part. This also applies to any verbal agreements made as you continue working together. Besides the fact that the shareholders' agreement is a legally binding document, it is also just common courtesy to stick to your word.

Minor changes and adjustments occur, but both parties must agree on them. More drastic changes to the deal or to the shareholders' agreement can have a bigger impact on the business, not to mention on the owner-successor relationship. Such changes may require formal agreement from both parties, and any existing legal documents should be updated to reflect them, so that there is no confusion in the future.

Ensure Clarity

Ensuring clarity when it comes to expectations, roles, and responsibilities is an all-around good rule for every facet of business—not just during a transition. Apply this approach to every meeting, agreement, and daily interaction, and you will avoid unnecessary conflict resulting from misunderstandings.

When we created our own transition plan, we met with our team to go over the details and ensure that everybody was aware of how it was to unfold. Once we came to an agreement, we started the process and went on our way. It was almost a year later, at our first annual succession meeting, when my dad raised a question about the value of the deal, which brought our transition to a halt. He had been under the impression that the agreed-upon value of the deal was about 20 percent more than originally understood. So there we were, over a year into the transition process, when it became apparent that we did not have clarity over the agreement we had made. And although we had a transition plan in place, we did not yet have our SA completed, so not all of the details had been finalized.

This was an obvious misstep on our part, which is why I strongly advise you to ensure that the transition plan and SA are both ready by the time the deal is made. Fortunately, with the support of our transition team we reviewed the previous meeting notes to discover that my dad had been mistaken and we clarified the true value of the deal.

The lesson here is to always ensure that everybody involved is clear about what is being discussed or agreed upon. In our case, there wasn't any malicious intent on either side to try and change the deal. Rather, a simple mistake was made because we did not have the SA completed.

Exhibit Professional Conduct

Maintaining professional conduct while in the workplace will help solidify both parties' roles as partners and reduce the likelihood of the parent-child dynamic stirring up conflict. Although they may always demonstrate parent-like tendencies toward their successor, the exiting owner should try to suppress such tendencies when dealing with business-related issues. When at work, treat all issues professionally. Keep discussions behind closed doors and out of earshot of staff. Ideally such conversations should be held outside of the workplace.

For many years, my dad and I would at times treat our office like our living room since we spent most of our time there. We would focus on work, but during lunch or in the afternoons we would loosen up and revert back to our father-son dynamic. This could be good at times because it lightened the atmosphere in the office, but that was also part of the issue, especially since we had an open-concept office layout, which meant everyone could hear our discussions, our laughter, and our disagreements.

As you can imagine, it was difficult to wear the hat of a partner and business owner while also being treated like a child. It was not a good look for either of us, and it is no surprise that it commonly resulted in some form of disagreement. Eventually both of us realized that we needed to change how we did things as our staff would not benefit from a divided leadership. Even during times of peace, our familial relationship had an effect on the staff as they too would adopt this relaxed approach while in the office. We ultimately came to the understanding that any family-type interactions would be best saved for outside of the office. Luckily, our office was next to a public park alongside a river, which made for a convenient location to carry our discussions freely.

Working toward achieving professional conduct in the office will help solidify both parties' roles within the company as leaders and help to avoid the unneeded familial conflicts while at the office. This, in turn, will set the tone for the company culture in general.

Foster Mutual Respect

As the exiting owner continues to offload their responsibilities to their successor, it is important for them to limit their interference with the business operations that are now the successor's responsibility. And likewise, the successor needs to be patient and respect that some things are still under the exiting owner's control.

It is not uncommon for the exiting owner to try to handle something on their own even though the task is clearly set for the successor. By this point, handling things will come as second nature to an experienced business owner, and they will have to check their impulse to exert control. Likewise, as the successor is looking to absorb more responsibility and assert their control over the company, they may step into the exiting owner's jurisdiction. Mutual respect needs to be exercised as both partners navigate the process of working out their own roles and responsibilities within the company.

During our own transition process, after I had moved out of the accounting department and had hired someone to fill the position, I still kept control over the higher-level financial functions of the business, such as approving payments and payroll. Money was still tight at times, and every dollar had to be allocated accordingly, so managing cash flow required a great deal of focus on my part.

As successor and exiting owner navigate their changing roles, mutual respect is key.

At the time, my dad still had his company credit card and would charge expenses without giving me a heads-up. The act of him using the card was not the issue; it was that I was not informed of certain purchases that could affect our company's cash flow.

I approached the issue with him and shared my side of it and how it had an impact on the company, which allowed him to see how it was affecting my ability to do the job. From then on we would communicate more regularly; I was able to more accurately project our cash flow needs while allowing him to use the card as required.

Rely on Your Transition Team

This one goes without saying, as I have already established the importance of putting together a reliable transition team. However, it warrants another mention as we can sometimes be too proud, or even forget, to seek the support of the people who can help us in times of need. If and when the moment arises that conflict between the partners is so pronounced that no progress is being made, relying on the help of your transition team will be necessary. Whether you seek out your business consultant, your lawyer, or your accountant, it is important to get an outside perspective on the issue at hand.

With any luck, it never gets to this point, but if there is still no resolution, the transition team can refer to the shareholders' agreement, which outlines the actions that can be taken to rectify a disagreement. Of course, this addresses only the legality of the matter and will not necessarily mend familial disagreements. But sometimes the simple act of listening to someone else's perspective can be enough to help you see the light.

As I mentioned, our accountant filled this role of consultant for us. I'm not sure this is something all accountants are able to do, but ours in particular was quite invested in our succession, and I believe he genuinely wanted to help us in whatever way he could. As a result, he was able to support us not only by providing his accounting services, but also by acting as the mediator. Without having a third party mediate conflict between my dad and me, our succession would not have gone as well as it did.

Communicate through Planned Meetings

One of the most effective ways to avoid conflict between partners is to ensure open communication about the direction of the business and each party's intentions for the future. This is easily accomplished by holding scheduled business planning meetings. These meetings help keep everyone informed of what is to come, and provide an open forum for discussion of key business issues. This is especially important as the successor takes on more of the leadership role and steers the direction of the business. During these meetings, make sure to involve your transition team, or at least the core members, and be consistent with who attends year after year.

Depending on the complexity of your transition, or what stage you are at, you could have as many meetings as you determine is required. We started off by having two meetings per year: one for reviewing the year-end financials of the business, which was always around July or

August, and another to discuss and review the actual transition process, which was usually in December or January.

These meetings are critical for the exiting owner to get a sense of how the transition is going and how the business is performing. If they let go too quickly without verifying that the successor is capable of the task, it can of course cause issues for everybody involved. For instance, let's say that for some reason your successor begins to steer the business in a radically different direction, putting both the company and your retirement at risk. In this case, you would certainly want to know what was going on sooner rather than later. The exiting owner needs to protect their interests and make sure that the business and its operations are healthy and able to continue as planned. Meeting regularly will ensure that both the exiting owner and the successor are striving toward the same objectives.

During one of our year-end meetings, after we'd had a couple of back-to-back outstanding years, our accountant asked for my thoughts on what would be the next step for the business. My answer was "expansion!" I wanted to keep growing, which at the current rate would mean that we would need a second or larger facility, more people, and more infrastructure—all to the tune of more costs. My dad instantly perked up when he heard my response. He knew that expansion could put a strain on the business,

> **Regular meetings between exiting owner and successor will keep focus on shared objectives.**

which in turn could affect the transition process. With a worried look on his face, he advised the team that we should have everything well planned out before doing anything of the sort. Now, I wasn't saying we were going to expand in an unplanned or haphazard way, but still, his concern was natural, and it ultimately raised my awareness of how the direction of the business could affect him.

We discussed my plans for expansion even though I hadn't fully planned out the details. I was excited about our recent growth and wanted to keep it going. After discussing my ideas with our team and putting some more thought into the matter, we agreed that we would continue growing but at a controlled rate and with a focus on efficiencies and stabilization before planning any big expansion. It was the right decision, and what's important is that we made it as a team.

During your meetings you should thoroughly discuss all business financials, challenges, and other relevant matters that will have a direct impact on the business. Doing so will give the exiting owner a good snapshot of what they may have missed. These meetings are also the time to discuss and review the details of the transition process pertaining to the redemption of shares, ownership stakes, voting rights, and related issues. Attending these meetings gave me a sense of accomplishment, providing the opportunity to reflect on my progress. I could see the shares I was buying out every year and that reinforced my sense of ownership and commitment as successor.

As the exiting owner continues to step away from the daily operations, these meetings will become their window into the business, offering them a chance to verify that all is going according to plan. Although my dad and I talk on a weekly basis, we don't always discuss business, and the times we do are usually brief conversations without getting into the details. This is why attending a couple of meetings a year gives him assurance that the business is healthy and progressing.

Communication is key to ensuring a successful transition. The channels need to be wide open from the beginning as both parties learn to work together as partners and co-owners. After many years, my dad and I found a rhythm for communicating with each other—one based solely on trust.

In the beginning of our transition my dad wanted frequent updates on how the business was doing and whether there were any challenges or issues that needed his attention. As a result we held meetings on a regular basis. However, as time went by and our trust grew, meetings and updates became less frequent because my dad had learned to rely on me. We even developed a short form of updating one another. Whenever we would talk, be it a quick phone conversation or over a family dinner, my dad would just ask, "How's the business? All good?" I would reply, "Yep. All good." and the business conversation would end there. We got to a level of trust with each other where he understood that me saying that everything was good meant that he needn't worry. If something wasn't "all good," I would tell him about it. Having this level of trust in each other has allowed us to fulfill our roles in the transition process without having to constantly double check with one another.

Keeping lines of communication open and attending scheduled business planning meetings will ensure that the exiting owner and successor are on the same page and working toward the same goal, which ultimately helps avoid potential conflicts.

CHAPTER 12

Enjoy the Journey

As the exiting owner frees themself from the responsibilities of running the business, they should endeavour to enjoy their newfound freedom. When I say "enjoy the journey," I mean just that—your role as the exiting owner is taking you to a new stage in life, one that you've worked hard for.

During our own transition I found that the last couple of years of working together were some of the toughest times for our partnership. I was eager and ready to lead, but my dad was still actively involved in the business and had not come to grips with the fact that it was time to settle into a new life.

Many exiting owners and successors will encounter similar situations: the successor has become capable of running the business, but the previous owner has not yet stepped back, leading to a redundancy in leadership. By this point, the previous leader's role should have evolved to overseeing, assessing, and guiding the successor as opposed to working directly on the business. It may take the exiting owner years to get to the point that they feel comfortable enough to let go, but as their successor continues to prove themself and their abilities, they should be rewarded with the trust of letting go.

During these years, I made an effort to prove to my dad that I did indeed have things under control, and I was capable of leading the business. Even then, he had a hard time. That was understandable as succession is not marked with a date and a time as to when it will occur. Rather it is a gradual process. Although in theory the transition of ownership has a scheduled timeline, the position of business leader can be earned anytime during that process.

> **Succession is a process of continuous improvement.**

Over time, my dad realized we were doing great things together, and that our formula was working. The less he did, the more I was able to take on, and that fueled my desire to succeed. When we got to this point in the journey, I could see that he found pleasure and pride in being able to coach me and see my success. Our relationship as partners, and as father and son, drastically improved. The tension we had once experienced seemed to melt away once we were able to settle into our new roles.

Enjoying the journey doesn't mean the exiting owner is no longer part of the business and that they can begin living a new life at the flip of a switch. As time passes, other activities and interests will take your focus off the business's day to day activities, and you will be able to explore new chapters in your life. When my dad became more comfortable with letting me run the business, I could see that he was able to enjoy the journey. He became more involved in the Rotary Club, philanthropic activities, fishing, and travelling—interests that helped him develop a new identity.

As the exiting owner you want to be the one making the choices as to how the years ahead will play out and not have them decided for you. That said, it is hard to time things perfectly. If you decide to wait for the right time to let go of your business, you may be waiting for a long while.

In business, you rarely get a guarantee of anything. You do your best to stack the odds in your favour, you follow your intuition, and you take your chances. But there is always some risk that whatever chance you take may not work out. In the case of succession, the risk is a calculated one. You have prepared for this moment. All that is left is to take that leap!

Part of enjoying the journey means learning to be grateful and content with what you have accomplished. Take pride in the fact that you are achieving what few other family businesses are able to do; that is, surviving another generation. You did it with your family. You have given your successor an amazing opportunity to create a life of their own within the business, one that will support you, your successor, and your family for years and hopefully for more generations to come. Celebrate your successes and allow yourself to enjoy the rest of the journey.

The Ensuring Success Phase: Key Points

Ensuring success is the final phase in the transition journey. The focus of this phase, as its name suggests, is to ensure success during and after the transition of ownership. Succession is not a one-time event that occurs overnight. Instead, it is a gradual process that will take many years to complete, through which family harmony must be maintained.

To ensure success through this process, the exiting owner must begin by understanding how to redefine yourself as you back away from your business. Perhaps, as is the case for many business owners, your identity is largely tied with your business. However, you are now moving into a new life that is not defined by your business role. Your role during this phase—even though it may appear to be diminishing—is still very important to the transition. The business needs to learn to function without your presence and direct input, and your successor needs to be able to take over the reins, exhibiting the leadership qualities required.

All sorts of things can hinder your ability to fully let go, which in turn can delay the transition process. You may need to look at your situation, find the sticking points, and address them accordingly. Remember that your successor does not have the many years of business experience that you do, and they will require your ongoing support and patience. As the reality of letting go settles in, you need to shift your attention to simply being there for your successor. A great successor looks for ways of bringing further value to the business, strives for personal development, and stays in tune with changes in the industry and market. A great predecessor provides support and encouragement in any way they can while remaining hands-off.

Eventually, you will arrive at a point in time when you can ask yourself the question "Who's the boss now?" and know that the answer is your successor.

CONCLUSION

Achieving Transition Success

Given the nature of family businesses, relationships between family members should be of utmost importance. A transition that results in a transfer of ownership but causes division in the family is not my idea of a successful transition. I would suspect it's not yours either. Through the use of the strategies outlined above, the exiting owner and the successor will be able to develop a better working relationship with one another and communicate in a manner that helps support a positive transition.

Transition success for us came at many different stages in the journey, not just at the end. Each milestone reached was its own achievement as we knew we were getting closer to our end goal. The good and bad times that we faced taught us necessary lessons to become a stronger family entity. It was that process of learning to work together, discovering each other's strengths and weaknesses, that allowed us to build a family bond that is now stronger than ever.

Before you know it, the succession process will have reached its conclusion. Achieving transition success means that you have reached the point in time where the business is now owned and operated by the successor while family unity has also been maintained.

As you recall, the original transition plan that my dad and I had in place allowed for the transfer of ownership to be done over a period of ten years. In the end, however, through the use of the strategies and experiences shared in this book, we were able to complete the transfer of ownership in a fraction of the time.

The first five years of our plan were front-loaded; my dad received about 70 percent of the deal's value during this time, leaving only 30 percent to be redeemed over the final five years. This approach opened up a new opportunity for the business. Four and half years into the deal, we met with our transition team to go over the business's year-end financials. By this point, the business was about three times larger than it had been when we'd originally started the transition, which allowed me to start saving some profit either for a rainy day or to fund further expansion plans.

Our accountant was thrilled that we were in such a healthy financial position, which led him to bring up the idea of buying out the remaining shares and completing our succession five years ahead of schedule. Now, at this point both my dad and I knew that we could either increase or decrease the timeline of the buyout as we needed, but we hadn't noticed or even discussed that a buyout of this sort would be an option so soon. We discussed the possibility, how it would work and what it would mean for my dad and me. In short, my dad would receive the rest of the amounts owed to him in one lump sum and I would become the sole shareholder of the business.

As much as I was interested in this idea, it was still a considerable sum of money that I would need to part with. Naturally I was a bit slower at writing the cheque! Likewise, my dad also had his own thoughts as his scheduled income for the next five years would no longer be in place and he would have to adjust his plans accordingly.

After thinking over this new and exciting idea, we concluded that it was indeed feasible for us to take this approach given that we had the financing available and doing so would finalize the entire succession process in a clean and direct way. With the two of us in agreement, our transition team prepared the appropriate documents. I wrote the cheque, and we both signed on the dotted line. Our journey of transitioning the family business from one generation to the next had finally reached its conclusion. We both came out of the meeting happier than ever. We hugged, went for lunch, reminisced on the years past, and realized what we had just achieved.

Looking back at it now, I know that we wouldn't have been able to achieve this within the same time frame, had we not followed the path laid out in this book. I wrote Secrets to Succession in a way that would give you the reader an overview of the entire succession process in aims for you to be better prepared for the journey ahead.

The strategies and concepts I've shared are candidly pulled directly from our own experience to help you manoeuvre the most common challenges and pitfalls. By approaching the process of succession in phases, you can address this overwhelming task in a sequential manner that will support future progress and get you one step closer to transition success.

As you may have realized by now, the most challenging parts in a family business transition pertain mostly to the inter-family dealings. The ability to work with one another, through the good times and the bad is what will ultimately allow the business to succeed. A united family working toward a common goal is able to overcome any challenge.

AFTERWORD

As Gerard's father, the biggest challenge in the succession process for me was coming to grips with the fact that I needed to exit the business at some point. When I was completely absorbed by the daily operations of the business and making everything work, it was easy to ignore future plans for an exit strategy. But when I was diagnosed with cancer, I realized quickly that some kind of succession plan needed to be made, and that at some point I would need to exit the business. My hope was that my son, Gerard, would take over.

After I went into remission, I made the effort to begin the plans for succession even though it would be ten or more years into the future. Working alongside Gerard was very rewarding. But needless to say, it was at times challenging and required a lot of patience, especially during the earlier years when Gerard was still learning how the business operated and he was acquiring the skills to become a manager and a leader.

Grooming my successor in the way that I did—bringing him into the business at an early age, and instilling a work ethic, values, and attributes that I thought were important—helped with the transition of the business and his outlook on life in general.

Relying on our transition team was central to our success. Having the right team in place allowed us to plan accordingly. They provided support when needed, and helped mitigate conflict.

Not all went smoothly, of course. We had to figure out how to navigate the actual creation of the transition plan and all the complicated legal planning that went along with it. I had a good understanding as to how to groom Gerard to take over the business, but when it came to the actual details of how ownership would transfer over to him, I had to learn as we went along, and so I let our transition team handle most of that.

During the development and execution of the shareholders' agreement we did not see eye-to-eye, and I think we could have done that better. It caused a lot of issues for us, and had we known a better way or what to expect, we could have saved many arguments and years of trying to figure it out.

As a "big picture" guy, I did not concern myself with the finer details and inner workings of the transition plan and shareholders' agreement, whereas Gerard, also new to the process, looked at it from a detailed point of view, which naturally caused friction between us. We were not on the same page during this process. Not knowing what we were getting ourselves into or how to go about it in the right way was the main reason we had so many challenges during this stage of succession.

Now that I'm fully retired, I do miss the social aspects of being around the office and interacting with our clients, but I don't miss it enough to want to return to work. Not having to worry about the business allows me to enjoy the time that I have now. I have the freedom to do what I want, whether it be fishing, golf, travel, or just relaxing. I like the freedom to choose to do whatever I want, when I want.

I am still friends with several of the company's long-standing employees. When I see them at our monthly poker game and they bring up how well Gerard and the business are doing, I feel a huge sense of pride and joy over everything we have done and what is now being accomplished. It is great to see that the business is doing as well as it is now that it is in its second generation of family ownership.

Through the lens of experience, I can make recommendations for when the time comes to stepping away from your business: love your successor and make your best efforts to find a path that benefits both of you. In order for the team to win, both the existing owner and successor have to win.

Groom and educate your successor and acknowledge their education, abilities, and ambitions. I knew when Gerard went to study business in university that he would be coming back with a new way of thinking, and I had to take this into account and see how we could incorporate his new knowledge into the team and the business.

Eventually, after working together for many years, you will learn to trust each other, settle into your respective roles, and begin working together as partners toward the same goals instead of pulling in different directions as you may have done in the past as parent and child.

At some point in your business succession, you will need to loosen the reins and allow your successor to lead the business. Be there for them during that time and offer your guidance and mentorship. It is only once you begin stepping back that your successor will truly be able to exercise their own leadership.

Several years after I had stepped back from the business, I was no longer going into the office on a regular basis. I received a knock at my door one day, and when I opened it, Gerard was standing on my doorstep; he had brought a box full of my office knickknacks and pictures that I had kept on my desk. He had cleaned out my old office and had finally made it his own. Although initially I was not too thrilled about this, I later realized that this was a good thing. He was signalling that he had taken over the ownership and responsibility for the business and I knew it was finally time to exit the stage.

There is a quote I've repeated for many years. Although I don't remember where I got it from, it still rings true: "When you are on a winning team, the only thing to do is to keep winning." This is especially true when you are on the path of succession. You must be able to continue working together, embrace each other's new roles, and stay the course until you reach your goal. Allow yourself to keep winning.

Robert Wolfe
January 2019

ACKNOWLEDGEMENTS

To my mom and sister, your love and support have encouraged me to be the best that I can be.

To my dad, thank you for helping me become an entrepreneur and giving me the opportunity of a lifetime to become a second-generation business owner.

I will be forever grateful.

BIBLIOGRAPHY

Aronoff, Craig E., and John L. Ward. *Family Business Governance: Maximizing Family and Business Potential*. New York, NY: Palgrave MacMillan, 2011.

Aronoff, Craig E., Stephen L. McClure, and John L. Ward. *Family Business Succession: The Final Test of Greatness*. New York, NY: Palgrave MacMillan, 2011.

Aronoff, Craig E., and Mary F. Whiteside. *How Families Work Together*. New York, NY: Palgrave MacMillan, 2011.

Bork, David. *The Little Red Book of Family Business*. Sampson Press, 2008.

Daughtery, Mary S., and Ernesto J. Poza. Family Business, 4th Edition. Cengage Learning, 2014.

Davis, John A., Kelin E. Gersick, Marion McCollom Hampton, and Ivan Lansberg. *Generation to Generation: Life Cycles of the Family Business*. Boston, MA: Harvard Business Review Press, 1997.

Ellis, David K. *Planning For Family Business Transition: A Practical Guide to Financial Health & Family Wealth*. Bloomington, IN: Author House, 2017.

Fleming, Quentin J. *Keep the Family Baggage Out of the Family Business: Avoiding the Seven Deadly Sins That Destroy Family Businesses*. New York: Touchstone, 2000.

Bibliography

Hutcheson, Henry. *Dirty Little Secrets of Family Business: Ensuring Success From One Generation to the Next.* Austin, TX: Greenleaf Book Press, 2016.

Long, Randy M. *The Braveheart Exit: 7 Steps to Your Family Business Legacy.* Las Vegas, NV: Next Century Publishing, 2016.

Pellegrin, Jonathan. *The Art of Selling the Family Business.* CreateSpace Independent Publishing Platform, 2017.

Werdiger, David. *Transition: How to Prepare Your Family and Business for the Greatest Wealth Transfer in History.* Canby, OR: Lasting Press, 2017.

ADDITIONAL READING

Cardone, Grant. *The 10X Rule: The Only Difference Between Success and Failure*. Hoboken, NJ: Wiley, 2011.

Cardone, Grant. *If You're Not first, You're Last: Sales Strategies to Dominate Your Market and Beat Your Competition*. Hoboken, NJ: Wiley, 2010.

Collins, Jim. *Good to Great: Why Some Companies Make the Leap and Others Don't*. New York, NY: Harper Business Books, 2001.

Collins, Jim, and Jerry I. Porras. *Built to Last: Successful Habits of Visionary Companies*. New York, NY: Harper Business Books, 2002.

Deans, Thomas W. *Every Family's Business: 12 Common Sense Questions to Protect Your Wealth*. Orangeville, ON: Detente Financial Press, 2008.

Eker, T. Harv. *Secrets of the Millionaire Mind: Mastering the Inner Game of Wealth*. New York, NY: HarperCollins, 2005.

Gerber, Michael E. *The E-Myth Revisited: Why Most Small Businesses Don't Work and What to Do About It*. New York, NY: HarperCollins, 1995.

Griffiths-Hamilton, Emily. *Build Your Family Bank: A Winning Vision for Multigenerational Wealth*. Vancouver, BC: Figure 1 Publishing, 2014.

Kiyosaki, Robert T, and Sharon L. Lechter. *Rich Dad Poor Dad*. Scottsdale, AZ: Plata Publishing, 1997.

Kiyosaki, Robert T, and Sharon L. Lechter. *Rich Kid Smart Kid: Giving Your Child a Financial Head Start*. New York, NY: Warner Business, 2001.

ABOUT THE AUTHOR

Gerard Gust is the President and CEO of Incredible Restorations, a multi-million-dollar family-owned property restoration company specializing in emergency and repair services.

Growing up in the family business, from childhood through university, Gerard was groomed to one day take over and handle the family's operation.

For over a decade, he worked alongside his dad as part of a father and son team. By the age of 27 he was able to earn the leadership position, expedite his dad's retirement plans, and take the company into its second generation of ownership.

About the Author

Having completed the succession process, Gerard shares his experience and knowledge in a way that both an exiting owner and successor can relate with in aims to help families in similar situations.

Gerard Gust lives in Vancouver, British Columbia, Canada.

Made in the USA
Columbia, SC
12 June 2024